INVADING
BABYLON

DESTINY IMAGE BOOKS BY THESE AUTHORS

Bill Johnson

A Life of Miracles
Dreaming With God
Center of the Universe
Momentum
Release the Power of Jesus
Strengthen Yourself in the Lord
The Supernatural Power of a Transformed Mind
Hosting the Presence

Lance Wallnau

Turn the World Upside Down

Alan Vincent

The Good Fight of Faith
Heaven on Earth

C. Peter Wagner

Let's Laugh
Warfare Prayer
Praying with Power

Patricia King

Spiritual Revolution
Dream Big

INVADING BABYLON

THE 7 MOUNTAIN MANDATE

BILL JOHNSON | LANCE WALLNAU

ALAN VINCENT | C. PETER WAGNER
CHÉ AHN | PATRICIA KING

DESTINY IMAGE® PUBLISHERS, INC.

P.O. Box 310, Shippensburg, PA 17257-0310

"Promoting Inspired Lives."

This book and all other Destiny Image, Revival Press, MercyPlace, Fresh Bread, Destiny Image Fiction, and Treasure House books are available at Christian bookstores and distributors worldwide.

For a U.S. bookstore nearest you, call **1-800-722-6774.**

For more information on foreign distributors, call **717-532-3040.**

Reach us on the Internet: **www.destinyimage.com.**

ISBN 13 TP: 978-0-7684-0335-0

ISBN 13 Ebook: 978-0-7684-8566-0

For Worldwide Distribution, Printed in the U.S.A.

7 8 9 / 21 20 19

CONTENTS

THE KINGDOMS OF
THIS WORLD HAVE BECOME
THE KINGDOMS OF OUR LORD
AND OF HIS CHRIST,
AND HE SHALL REIGN
FOREVER AND EVER!
—REVELATION 11:15

INTRODUCTION

*Surely the Lord God does nothing, unless
He reveals His secret to His servants the
prophets.*—Amos 3:7

Someone once said that it is the responsibility of every believer
to discover what God is doing in his or her generation and to
partner with His divine plan. The question then becomes, how
do we discover what God is doing in this hour and how do we
partner with that plan? As we listen to the prophetic voices in
our generation, we discover what God is doing in our midst so
we can co-labor with Him to see His Kingdom come.

It is our great honor at Destiny Image to publish books
that offer the body of Christ relevant, anointed, and engaging
content. We often choose to publish books that we consider
to be "now words" for the Church, so when several authors
write on the same topic, we take note. When multiple authors
from various places around the world submit manuscripts that
teach a variation of the same message, it is clear to us that God

is pouring out a timely Word for the body that deserves special attention.

Invading Babylon is a collection of teachings from some of today's most anointed and prophetic voices. Each chapter offers a different perspective on relevant ways to infiltrate and influence our society with Christian values and standards. Leaders around the world are discovering that lasting cultural transformation only occurs when the Gospel infiltrates every aspect of society. God is pouring out specific strategies to invade our culture, so that we can see complete cultural transformation. We need to see godly, anointed believers bringing a heavenly perspective into the business sector, into schools, into politics, and into the arts. Ministry isn't just for pastors; every believer has a special calling, anointing, and gift that they can use to display the goodness of God to the world. This message is not brand new. In fact, it first started circulating almost 40 years ago, and yet it is just as relevant today as it was yesterday.

Bill Johnson, senior leader of Bethel Church in Redding, California, opens this book with a foundational teaching on dominion theology. In simple terms, dominion theology is the idea that Christian believers are called to not only preach the Gospel and win converts to Christ but also to establish the Kingdom of God on the earth. Bill encourages all believers to learn how to walk in the full authority of the Gospel so they can heal the sick, raise the dead, and see people touched and transformed by the power of God. One must believe that we are *all* called to minister to the world, regardless of our titles and vocations, as this supernatural lifestyle is a *natural* part of the Christian life. Miraculous ministry is not just for pastors, evangelists, and missionaries. It is for everyone.

Many believers do not believe they are called to full-time ministry because they do not feel called to preach on Sunday mornings, but ministry should extend beyond the four walls of the Church. Take, for example, the life of Stephen. After the Church was born, the apostles devoted themselves to preaching the Gospel, but they were so focused on preaching the Word of God that other needs were neglected.

> *Now in those days, when the number of the disciples was multiplying, there arose a complaint against the Hebrews by the Hellenists, because their widows were neglected in the daily distribution. Then the twelve summoned the multitude of the disciples and said, "It is not desirable that we should leave the word of God and serve tables. Therefore, brethren, seek out from among you seven men of good reputation, full of the Holy Spirit and wisdom, whom we may appoint over this business; but we will give ourselves continually to prayer and to the ministry of the word." And the saying pleased the whole multitude. And they chose Stephen, a man full of faith and the Holy Spirit* (James 6:1-5).

Stephen was chosen to help run the food bank that supplied food to the widows among them. At first glance this task does not appear to be very spiritual in nature, but Stephen was chosen because he was full of faith and the Holy Spirit. Some might see Stephen's assignment as a demotion; he wasn't chosen to teach the Word or travel and preach, and yet God used Stephen mightily among those he served. He found his supernatural calling in the midst of a natural career.

> *And Stephen, full of faith and power, did great wonders and signs among the people....And they were not able to resist the wisdom and the Spirit by which he spoke* (Acts 6:8, 10).

Stephen walked in the fullness of God right where he was and he made a tremendous impact on those around him. Stephen was essentially a glorified waiter, but he did not act like a waiter. No, he instead walked in signs and wonders and brought the influence of the King of kings wherever he went. Those around him were unable to resist the wisdom and Spirit that enabled him to speak. He gained such a reputation for spreading the Gospel that he received great persecution and became the first martyr. Stephen believed he was called to make a difference in his sphere of influence; his title and vocation didn't hinder him from engaging in full-time ministry. He took dominion over the area that was entrusted to him and established God's Kingdom in Jerusalem.

How does the Church invade Babylon? Just like Stephen did, by confidently infiltrating every area of life with the Kingdom of God. Lance Wallnau contributes the second chapter to this book and he offers us a divine understanding of how to embrace this naturally supernatural lifestyle. Lance has devoted his life to equipping the body of Christ with the knowledge of how to invade the world with the Kingdom. Lance shares the Seven Mountain revelation that Bill Bright, of Campus Crusade for Christ, and Loren Cunningham, founder of Youth With a Mission (YWAM), received almost 30 years ago.

The Seven Mountain revelation helps us strategically identify different aspects of society so that cultural transformation can become a manageable task. All of us are called to at least one of these seven mountains: religion, arts, media, business, government, family, and education. When we relegate ministry to the religion mountain, we forfeit the opportunity to influence the rest of our culture. We wonder why movies, books, politics, schools, and families are lacking Christian values, and yet we do not empower believers who live and work in these realms to see themselves as active agents of change who can establish strongholds of truth and justice in the world. We need believers in positions of power—at the peaks of these mountains—in order to see our communities impacted by the presence of the King and His Kingdom. Lance's insights into the Seven Mountain revelation will change the way you view ministry and the call of God on your life.

As we begin taking land for our King, we will undoubtedly face great resistance. Prayer is our greatest weapon of warfare and will open doors and shift heavenly realms so that God's presence can be ushered into our communities. The third chapter of this book is from Alan Vincent's book, *The Kingdom at War.* Alan offers a profound teaching about taking spiritual ground by occupying the spiritual gates of our cities. Gates represent the spiritual powers that rule over geographical areas.

> *Be strong in the Lord and in the power of His might.... For we do not wrestle against flesh and blood, but against principalities, against powers, against the rulers of the darkness of this age, against spiritual hosts of wickedness in the heavenly places* (Ephesians 6:10, 12).

If we are to have any hope of reaching our world with the Gospel, we must understand that there is a spiritual component to influencing our world. We must first recognize demonic spiritual powers and displace them through prayer and fasting. This chapter will be invaluable to anyone who feels as if they are making no headway advancing the Kingdom.

C. Peter Wagner also brings great wisdom to this conversation about cultural transformation. He has been a forerunner in teaching about dominion theology and cultural transformation for years, and the fourth chapter of this book was originally published in his book, *The Reformer's Pledge*. Wagner identifies one of the reasons the Church has struggled with gaining momentum in cultural transformation: money. As the Church gains wisdom in acquiring and distributing finances, she will gain great favor and influence in the world.

We all know that money makes the world go 'round, but the Church often doesn't seem to have enough. Most local congregations host fundraisers every time they want to do something beyond the monthly budget. Youth groups wash cars for cash and adults make building pledges, but we need to learn how to gain and steward money more effectively. It is admittedly difficult to gain any momentum with cultural transformation if you need to raise special funds every time your church has a creative idea to reach your community. Wagner offers fresh insights and strategies about raising and stewarding finances so we can fund God's expanding Kingdom.

Ché Ahn takes the Seven Mountain mandate one step further by advocating for something beyond cultural transformation. He is committed to seeing cultural reformation. A reformation brings lasting change to a society. Consider, for example, the revolutionary and long-lasting effect of the Protestant Reformation.

After Martin Luther nailed his Ninety-Five Theses to the door of the Catholic Church, great changes started rippling throughout the Body of Christ. These changes, however, were not a temporary transformation. Luther's teachings set in motion a great rebellion against the Catholic Church, and the Protestant Church was born. Nearly 500 years later, the Protestant Church has influenced society and successfully established pillars of infrastructure so that it will continue to grow in the future. This is reformation.

In order to see lasting change in our communities, our revivals need to lead to transformation and to reformation. Ché Ahn offers incredible wisdom to believers on how to pray in long-lasting cultural change, so that the kingdoms of this world become the Kingdoms of our God (see Rev. 11:15).

The final chapter in this book illustrates the power of a believer who decides to invade a non-religious pillar of our society—the media mountain. Patricia King is a powerfully anointed prophetic voice to this generation and God called her to the world of television to share the Gospel and broadcast the Word of the Lord to the nations.

Patricia's story is incredible and it demonstrates God's faithfulness to open doors and back us up when we step out in faith. When we continue doing what we have always done, we will only accomplish what has already been accomplished. If we step out in faith according to what we know we are capable of doing, we never tap into the hidden resources God has placed within us or access the miracle-working power of God that is available to us through the anointing. Patricia's testimony of God's faithfulness as she stepped out in faith to infiltrate Hollywood and the world of television will stir you deeply. Embedded within her words is an impartation of divine life, for the testimony of Jesus is a literal prophetic promise to us, and we receive a corresponding anointing to carry out similar exploits.

> *For the testimony of Jesus is the spirit of prophecy* (Revelation 19:10).

Dear friends, God has called us to make disciples of all nations. We are to preach the Good News that God's Son came to save us and to welcome us into His family and His realm. We look to Jesus' life on earth as a perfect representation of God the Father's heart for us. Jesus healed the sick, raised the dead, breathed life into those around Him, and He declared justice and peace to the world. We are called to be His disciples and to bring His presence into our workplaces, our homes, our schools, our government, our media, our arts, and our religion. Let us embrace our call to invade Babylon and strategically bring the Kingdom of God into every aspect of society.

In order to understand
how to invade Babylon,
you must first understand
that you are called
and equipped to
invade Babylon.

INVADING BABYLON

Bill Johnson

*Any gospel that doesn't work in the
marketplace doesn't work.*

We have been given authority over this planet. It was first given to us in the commission God gave to mankind in Genesis (see Gen. 1:28-29) and was then restored to us by Jesus after His resurrection (see Matt. 28:18). But Kingdom authority is different than is typically understood by many believers. It is the authority to set people free from torment and disease, to destroy the works of darkness. It is the authority to move the resources of Heaven through creative expression to meet human need. It is the authority to bring Heaven to earth. It is the authority to serve.

As with most Kingdom principles, the truths of humanity's dominion and authority are dangerous in the hands of those who desire to rule over others. These concepts seem to validate some people's selfishness. But when these truths are expressed through the humble servant, the world is rocked to its core. Becoming servants to this world is the key to open the doors of possibility that are generally thought of as closed or forbidden.

Neither our understanding of servants or of kings can help us much with this challenge for both are soiled in our world, probably beyond repair. That is where Jesus comes in. He is the King of all kings, yet the Servant of all. This unique combination found in the Son of God is the call of the hour upon us. As truth is usually found in the tension of two conflicting realities, we have an issue to solve. Like our Master we are both royalty and servants (see Rev. 1:5; Mark 10:45). Solomon warns of a potential problem, saying, "the earth…cannot bear up: under a slave when he becomes king" (Prov. 30:21-22 NASB). Yet Jesus contradicted Solomon's warning, without nullifying the statement, by being effective at both. Jesus served with the heart of a king but ruled with the heart of a servant. This is the essential combination that must be embraced by those longing to shape the course of history.

Royalty is my identity. Servanthood is my assignment. Intimacy with God is my life source. So, before God, I'm an intimate. Before people, I'm a servant. Before the powers of hell, I'm a ruler, with no tolerance for their influence. Wisdom knows which role we are to fulfill at the proper time.

Invading the Mountains of Influence

There are seven realms of society that must come under the influence of the King and His Kingdom. For that to happen, we, as citizens of the Kingdom, must invade. The dominion of the Lord Jesus is manifest whenever the people of God go forth to serve by bringing the order and blessing of His world into this one.

The effort by many believers to simply obtain positions of leadership is putting the cart before the horse. Servanthood remains our strong suit, and through service we can bring the benefits of His world into the reach of the common man.

The Kingdom is likened unto leaven (see Matt. 13:33). As yeast has an effect on the dough it is "worked into," so we will transform all the kingdoms of this world as we are worked into its systems. From there we must display His dominion and rule. As the people of God move into these realms of society to show forth the benefits and values of the Kingdom, His government expands.

For this invasion to work effectively, we must correct a few misconceptions. In doing so, it is equally important to establish the necessary Kingdom principles in their proper order.

There is no such thing as secular employment for the believer. Once we are born again, everything about us is redeemed for Kingdom purposes. It is all spiritual. It is either a legitimate Kingdom expression, or we shouldn't be involved at all.

Every believer is in full-time ministry—only a few have pulpits in sanctuaries. The rest have their pulpit in their areas of expertise and favor in the world system. Be sure to preach only good news. And when necessary, use words!

The call of God is important, not because of the title it carries (or doesn't carry). It's valuable because of the One who called us. An assignment to be in business is as valuable in the Kingdom as is the call to be an evangelist. The privilege to be a stay-at-home wife and mother is equal in importance to being a missionary. Embrace your call with the faithfulness and thankfulness worthy of the One who has called you.

Our eternal rewards do not come because of how much money we made, how many souls were saved, or how many homeless people we fed. All rewards are given based on our faithfulness to what God has given and called us to be and to do. The honor we give to one another must not be only to those who have obvious spiritual occupations. Honor must be given to those who are faithful in the call, no matter what it is.

Prophetic ministry is not to be focused on the sins of the world. It takes very little discernment to find the dirt in people's lives. The prophetic in its purest form is designed to find the gold in people's lives and call it to the surface. This approach changes the attitude of the world toward the Church, and makes it possible for us to be contributors to society, not just confronters of all that is evil.

Covert vs. Overt Ministry

Our church and ministry school is most often known for its overt ministry—outward and aggressive. We have seen hundreds of people healed and delivered in public places. We've even had words of knowledge[1] given over the intercom of a local grocery store. The results were amazing. People responded by gathering around cash register number 10 and receiving the healing ministry of Jesus through one of our young men, Chad. Following God's merciful display of power, Chad invited the crowd to give their lives to Christ. Many did.

Overt ministry is very common for us. Whether it's in the mall, neighborhoods, schools, or places of business, the Gospel is brought to those in need. But this is only half of the needed ministry equation. The other half is covert ministry. The word covert means "hiding place." This refers to ministry that is subtler in nature. It is not hidden because of cowardice but rather out of wisdom. It works within the systems of this world to bring about change by reestablishing the proper norms of thoughts, beliefs, disciplines, and relational boundaries. In other words, we work to change the culture. This requires more time, as the goal is not a specific healing or conversion. The goal is the transformation of society itself by invading the systems of the city in order to serve. Serving for their benefit, not ours, is the key. As someone once said, "We shouldn't try to be the best in the world. We should try to be the best for the world!" When we set aside our religious agendas to make others a success, we have learned the Kingdom mindset and have become a part of the transformation movement.

Dumping Religious Agendas

The Church is sometimes known for its willingness to serve, but usually with well-meaning spiritual agendas as the ultimate goal. It almost sounds blasphemous, but serving simply to get people saved is a religious agenda. As pure and noble as it may seem to us as believers, it is manipulative to the world and is viewed as impure service. The world can smell it a mile away. We put them on the defensive when we carry such reasons for serving into their sphere of responsibility. But, for example, when we volunteer in our local school to help the principal succeed, then we've crossed the line into territory seldom visited by the Church. It is serving for the benefit of another. It's that kind of a servant whom the world welcomes. The amazing bonus is you also end up influencing the school in ways you never thought possible, including bringing people to Christ.

What would happen if parents volunteered in their local schools to help the teacher succeed? Generally teachers have an authentic interest in children succeeding in life. They invest themselves for the sake of another generation. They deserve honor for their commitment; and we can help them succeed.

School districts are accustomed to Christians seeking positions on local school boards. Sometimes Christian parents will work together to get a principal to change a particular curriculum or to fire a teacher because he or she is an atheist. But what would happen if we actually invaded the systems of this world to give honor where it is due, instead of dishonoring those whom we think deserve expulsion? The former brings transformation through favor. The latter is a self-fulfilling prophecy of rejection, as the world has few options but to protect what they are stewards over from the outside group (us) that wants to be in control. Christians are notorious for trying to take over schools through political maneuvering.[2] It may work from time to time, but it is neither the way of the Kingdom, nor will it prevail. There is a better way.

Interestingly enough, the fullness of the Spirit can also be seen in these two distinct approaches to ministry. The fullness of the Spirit makes way for believers who walk in wisdom, make practical contributions to the needs of society, and who also confront the impossibilities of life through the provisions of the Cross—solutions through supernatural display. Perhaps it is these two things working in tandem that should be considered the balanced Christian life.

The Seven Mind-Molders of Society

Both Dr. Bill Bright, founder of Campus Crusade for Christ, and Loren Cunningham, founder of Youth With A Mission, received the same revelation from God around the same period of time: there are seven major realms of influence in society that shape the way we live and think. Kingdom-oriented people must invade these mountains of influence in order for the transformation of society to take place. These mountains are:

- Home
- Church
- Education
- Media (Electronic and Print)

- Government & Politics
- Performing Arts (including Entertainment and Sports)
- Commerce (including Science and Technology).

It is interesting to note that God gave this insight to two men who lead significant youth movements. It is obvious that God wants an entire generation to value their call regardless of what title it brings, so He can teach them how to invade a culture for its total and complete transformation. God fully intends for there to be a fulfillment of His Word: "the kingdoms of this world are become the kingdoms of our Lord" (Rev. 11:15 KJV).

The following list is a little different from the original. It is not an improved list, but it does have a slightly different emphasis to more accurately represent our application of these principles. They are not listed in any order of importance.

- Business
- Education
- The Church
- Family
- Arts & Entertainment
- Science & Medicine
- Government

Wisdom is the vital ingredient to be effective in this invasion. I define wisdom with these three words: Integrity, Creativity, and Excellence. It is the display of the mind of God, always in the context of integrity, that brings forth the creative solutions for life, while holding to the standards of excellence. These play a vital role in manifesting the Kingdom in ways that honor God and solve the issues of life for humankind.

BUSINESS

Many Christians have tried to gain favor and position in the business world but have failed miserably. It is hard to gain favor in that world without prosperity. Prosperity is the primary measure for success in the business arena. With that in mind, the world is also full of stories of great financial success that were disasters in every other way. People instinctively want both—outward and inward success. The Kingdom businessperson has the chance to display a more complete picture of success by focusing on more than money. Their celebration of life, with all its many facets, will grab the attention of those hopelessly trapped in the "money is success" daily grind.

While there is room for overt ministry in every part of life, it is generally not the outward preaching of the Gospel that secures the place of favor in the eyes of the unbelieving businessperson. It is the divine (Kingdom) order a believer has in his or her overall approach to life—to self, family, business, and community.

Even the world knows that money is not the only measure of true success. Most of those in business want much more than money for their labors. Simple things like joy, a happy home life, recognition, and meaningful friendships are an important part of the life of true prosperity. John the Beloved referred to this as "prosperity of soul" (see 3 John 2). Mixed into this quest is the cry for significance. The Kingdom businessperson is poised to illustrate that element by their approach to life. We help define the favor of God that is upon the Kingdom businessperson through our extra efforts in world relief, our personal participation in helping the poor in our own cities, and through other projects that require giving and sacrifice.

One of our men sold cars at a local used car lot owned by believers. When a woman came in to buy a car, he noticed that she was very troubled. Through the direction of the Holy Spirit, he was able to minister to her quite profoundly. She opened up to God and received major healing in her heart. When they were through he told her, "Because you have opened up your heart to me, I cannot sell you a car. It would be unfair for me to do so. Instead I will introduce you to another salesman who will help you find the kind of car you are looking for." He was unwilling to come close to the possibility of taking advantage of this woman by selling her something when she had become emotionally vulnerable to him.

Kris Vallotton, my co-leader at Bethel Church, used to own an automobile repair shop and several car part stores. A man once stole some tires and rims from his shop. He didn't realize, however, that Kris knew he was the thief, and he brought his car in to Kris' repair shop. When that customer came in to pick up his car and pay his bill, Kris took him into his office and told him, "I know you stole my tires and rims. And to show you that I forgive you, I am giving you the work we did on your truck for free." The man went to his vehicle and sat in silence for about five minutes without doing anything; he just stared off into space. (Occasionally, a person receives a Gospel tract that they will never forget. This man received one stamped "Paid in Full.")

Then there is the humorous story of an employee wanting to get one of his workmates in trouble. He told his boss, "Every time I pass his office he's just staring out the window. He needs to be fired!" His boss responded, "Leave him alone! Just the other day he came up with an idea that saved us over $300,000—by just staring out that window."

Creativity is a necessary component for the Kingdom businessperson. It brings fresh ideas that keep adventure as a central part of their assignment. Witty inventions are going to increase in the Christian community, as God is using that expression of wisdom to bring about a transfer of wealth for Kingdom purposes.

"Do you see a man who excels in his work? He will stand before kings; He will not stand before unknown men" (Prov. 22:29 NKJV). This verse tells us two things. One, the result of lives pursuing excellence: they will influence the influencers. Two, kings demand excellence. Many compromise in this area to make a quick buck, but it is excellence that provides wealth for the long term. Kingdom wealth has no sorrow (see Prov. 10:22). Excellence is a Kingdom value, and is not to be confused with perfectionism, which is a counterfeit and comes from the religious spirit. One of the clearest paths of promotion is through excellence.

EDUCATION

Often times the Church reacts to the abuses of the world system and creates an error equal in danger to one we have rejected. This was never truer than in the realm of education. The Western mindset values reason as the only proper measure of truth, and this has undermined the Gospel. This worldview, which Paul battled in First Corinthians, has been embraced by our educational culture. It is anti-Christ in nature. The supernatural then becomes subject to the evaluation of ignorant people. But the solution to this problem is not to reject education; the answer is to invade. Our rejection removes us from our place of preservation as the salt of the earth (Matt. 5:13).

God is willing to debate anyone (see Isa. 1:18). He is very secure in His understanding and arguments. He also backs up His insights with evidence that will bear up under scrutiny. Invading the educational system is essential, as this mountain greatly shapes the minds and expectations of the younger generation. While it could be argued that entertainers today have a greater role in shaping the minds of the young, it is the educators who generally shape the minds of the entertainers in their way of thinking.

Our young people need to believe they will be able to live their entire lives on this earth, and plan accordingly. Get educated, married, have children, all with a Kingdom mindset.

Too many generations who experience the outpouring of the Spirit forfeit their desires for training and education in order to do "the Lord's work." As noble as that sounds, it comes from a misunderstanding of real ministry aided by the idea that we will be taken out of here at any moment. This is a tender subject, as we must be ready to be with the Lord at any given moment. But, as the Church regains the perspective that no job is secular for the believer, the esteem will return for the positions in society that had little value in prior generations. The desire for Heaven is right and healthy, but it must not replace our commission: "Your kingdom come. Your will be done, on earth as it is in heaven" (Matt. 6:10 NASB). We were not commissioned to look into the clouds for His coming (see Acts 1:11). We were commanded to "occupy" until He comes (Luke 19:13 KJV). Occupy is a military term. And according to Kingdom values, occupation is always for the purpose of advancement.

Our children must become educated to become educators. But that goal is not complete without the Kingdom mindset. We are sending them into dangerous territory to get their training. Choose their schools carefully. Each teacher who trains your child is a delegated authority—delegated by you. The Bible does not give the authority for training children to the government, no matter how noble their intent. It rests upon your shoulders, so pray, pray, pray, and educate, educate, educate.

We would never send our child to a restaurant where only one in ten die of food poisoning. Yet we do that daily in our educational system, with odds that are much worse than one in ten. We often send them out, unguarded, into a system that works to undermine faith and ultimately their relationship with God. The answer is not to withdraw from society and move into the mountains to preserve the family unit. The answer is to train and invade. Our training is superior to theirs if it's authentic, because it is driven by a personal relationship with God and includes transforming divine encounters.

As for the believers who are already in the educational system, bravo! Invade with a Kingdom mindset. Such a way of thinking provides the mooring needed to stay stable in storms and conflict. It also puts you in place to provide the answers to the dilemmas created by the inferior "Greek" mindset. Most bad ideas (including bad theology) are only one divine encounter away from oblivion. We owe people an encounter with God. And that is what you carry into that mountain of influence.

Most people in our culture unknowingly live under the influence of a dark kingdom. Yet they suffer with problems that have their answer in the Kingdom of God and the believer. Both wisdom and power are available to us that we might provide solutions from another world that meet their needs.

At Bethel Church, we have a waiting list of schools wanting us to be part of their after-school program. Why? We have come alongside to serve, not take over. The liberty that is given to our teams (presently seven schools a week) is really quite amazing. There are many who believe that what we are doing is impossible. And as long as the Church maintains an adversarial relationship with the educational system, it will remain impossible.

Throughout Scripture we see that when God's people step forward to serve, God backs it up with power. The schools are asking for our help. They face problems on a daily basis that were unheard of 30 years ago. It is our hour to invade, serve, and shine for His glory!

Moral values are the basis for integrity. And moral values are rooted in the character of God. The supernatural educator has access to a realm of stability that others don't have. That is not to say one has to be a believer to have integrity. Many unbelievers do. But the supernatural element available in the realm of character is reserved for those who have the Spirit of the resurrected Christ living in them. Young people need educators with integrity, but they also need those who believe in them. Calling out the treasure in a young person can mark them for good forever. Oftentimes such an educator plants a seed that another person will harvest, but that is the joy of this Kingdom—no words return void (see 1 Cor. 3:5-9 and Isa. 55:11).

We have a team of educators in our church who, through Kingdom principles, have tapped into ways of defeating learning disorders in many children. This creative expression came to them through divine inspiration. It is the result of people realizing they have legal access into the mysteries of the Kingdom, and that they have a responsibility to bring those secrets into play in the lives of those with great needs. This affects all the lives within their sphere of influence. There are answers to every problem we face. There are methods of training people that are far superior to what we know now. Kingdom-oriented people, who know who they are in Christ, will access these secrets for the benefit of all who are around them.

Excellence is more than exhorting students to get good grades. It is a gift from God that uses the full measure of resources from both the natural and spiritual realities. Some just seem to be good at everything, while others appear to have been absent the day gifts and talents were given out. In reality, each person has an area where God has gifted him or her to excel and it is a wise educator who discovers that area in a child. An excellent teacher will bring excellence out of the one who can't find it in him or herself.

Entertainment

Entertainment includes the arts, professional sports, and the media.

It wasn't too long ago that the world of entertainment was deemed so unholy that believers were forbidden to enter. The Church has often fallen to the notion that darkness is stronger than light. Entertainment is a mountain of influence that must be invaded. The indictment of that realm being "unholy" was accurate, but unfortunately, it is also a self-fulfilling prophecy—anywhere we do not invade becomes darker in our absence. We are the "light of the world" (Matt. 5:14). The realms of society that we fail to invade are hopelessly lost to darkness. Invasion is the responsibility of light.

This is a realm that ought to have edification as a primary objective. When it is perverted, it steals and plunders. But in its primary function, it creates. Recreation comes from this— re-creation! It must not only be creative, it must create.

Heaven has what we want. Every creative dream is fulfilled in Heaven. The great news is that we have access to that realm through prayers of faith. For example: there are sounds in Heaven that earth has never heard. When a musician taps into that reality and communicates that sound here, Heaven will have found agreement on the earth and will invade. All art finds its origins in the person of God; more specifically, it's found in His holiness. The Scripture says, "in the beauty of holiness" (Ps. 29:2). It's tragic that holiness gets such poor treatment from the people of God. It is God's nature, His person. Beauty pours forth from that one attribute (see 2 Chron. 20:21).

When I was growing up there were few Christians in this mountain of influence. Baseball was my love, and I only knew of two Christians in all of baseball. I'm sure there were more, but the point is it wasn't common. Today there are many teams that have a large percentage of genuine believers. The same is true of the arts. No field is left untouched. God is planting His last days' army in these strategic places of influence.

Mel Gibson's movie *The Passion of the Christ* is testimony to the turning that is taking place in this mountain. The doors of this realm are open wide, as creativity is at an all-time low. Immorality, jealousy, hatred, and revenge are poor substitutes for real creativity.

There's such a vacuum in the area of integrity in this mountain that all true Kingdom people will quickly stand out. However, we can't be nonchalant about the pressure to conform to worldly standards that the believer will face. Being a stumbling block to others has been become an art form for many. People receive justification for their own immoral lifestyles by getting others to fall morally. But for those who have true foundations, the sky is the limit. In a crisis, people will always turn to those who are stable. Integrity will be a beacon of light to those wandering through this land of disappointment and shame.

It might seem that creativity is where we have the biggest challenge in this mountain of influence. The opposite is true. Writers, designers, and the like have substituted sensuality for creativity. This has left a huge gap in the area of real originality. Anyone who has escaped the pressure to duplicate trash will automatically be positioned to create. Learning how to pray in the Spirit and soak in His presence will give great advantages to those wanting to invade this mountain. Heaven has what we're looking for. And you'll have to go there to get it. The best novels and plays have yet to be written. The most beautiful melodies to ever grace the human ear are yet to be discovered. Those with an ear for God, who are discovering the experience of "being seated in heavenly places," will have access to things no other generation has ever seen before.

Many have mistakenly thought that the devil has all the good music. He is not creative. Tragically, he receives credit for too many things, even by the Church. How is it that an ungodly person can write a beautiful piece of music or a brilliant script for a movie? How is it they can paint a masterpiece or design buildings that take our breath away? They were made in the image of God, and He doesn't remove that distinguishing feature when a person rebels against Him (see Rom. 11:29). In recent days, believers who have adopted the Kingdom mindset have caught up to, and in some cases surpassed, the world in the area of excellence and will continue to do so.

THE CHURCH

Jesus gave His disciples a warning about the potential influence of religion on the mind when He said, "Beware of the leaven of the Pharisees and the leaven of Herod" (Mark 8:15). The mentality of the Pharisee places God at the center of everything, but He is worshiped as an impersonal and power-less deity. Their God dwells mostly in the realm of theory and supposition. They excel at traditions that are convenient and reverence that is self-serving. But there is not much in the religious community that is actually from the Kingdom of God. It has a wide-open door for people with a renewed mind.

Many in the religious community have a lot of sincerity. And when they see someone who actually practices the purity and power from the pages of Scripture, something comes alive in them. They hope it's true. They just lack examples.

Kingdom-oriented people have great opportunities in the midst of great opposition. But the rewards are worth every risk.

People often measure success by the number of people who attend their services, the copies of books or CDs sold, or TV show ratings. One of the most common fears in this world of influence is that "someone will steal my sheep." Being committed to another leader's success, with no personal agenda for gain, is essential for invasion into this mountain. Ignoring the external measurements of success will enable leaders to value what the King values—passion, purity, power, and people.

Compassion is one of the greatest tools we possess to invade this mountain of influence. One of the churches in our network wanted to touch a local Catholic orphanage. They live in a country where Protestants and Catholics do not work together. In fact, they are known for preaching against one another from their pulpits. When the pastor went to the priest to talk, the priest was naturally guarded. Yet the pastor worked hard to share with him that they wanted the opportunity to honor them for their heart for the orphans. He noted that they were doing something important that none of the Protestants had been willing to do. The pastor asked if there was anything the children needed. The priest told them of their need for shoes. In spite of their very limited resources, the Protestant church bought shoes for each child. The sacrifice needed for this particular church family to do such a thing is beyond what I can write about on these pages, yet they made it. From this simple act of love, the entire Church in this region has been rocked by this display of an authentic Gospel. A city is being healed from the religious animosity that has ruled over that area for decades.

The area of morality and integrity should be the area in which we have little problem. But that is not the case. While I don't believe the statistics that claim the Church (authentic believers) is equal to the world in divorce and immorality, the numbers are admittedly far too high. Divine encounters, accurate teaching from Scripture, and accountability to other members of the Body can help change this problem. Righteous people can provide righteous peer pressure. When fellowship becomes valuable enough that it is sacrificial, then those in fellowship begin to walk openly in the light—with integrity and accountability. (See Heb. 13:15-16.)

The Church is known for its ruts not its new ideas. Thankfully a great transformation is taking place in that area. While change for change's sake is not always healthy, those resistant to change are usually resistant to the Holy Spirit. If anyone should be known for creativity, it should be those in whom the accurate image of the Creator has been formed—born-again believers. There are better ways of doing things. Always. The Church is in the place of leading the way. Cultural relevance is rightfully the cry of the hour, but it must be relevance with power!

The Church has often taken the low road in the realm of excellence because of a misunderstanding of humility. The choice of that road, however, usually flows from low faith, and humility gets the blame. Excellence can and must be the expression of true humility as humility declares, "Our best, for His glory!" Most of the areas that can bring the greatest results have the greatest risk. This is no exception. Excellence is Kingdom. Perfectionism is religion. Poverty is demonic.

FAMILY

The pressure being exerted on the family today makes this one of the easiest and most important areas to invade. Even those who seem to work overtime to destroy the family unit instinctively hunger for healthy relationships, significance, and a legacy. All a family needs to do to have influence in this mountain is to be healthy and not hidden. When relationships are good, and the boundaries of godly disciplines are intact, there is no limit to the influence of the Christian home. The problem has often been a false standard of holiness wherein the Christian doesn't associate with the unbeliever, yet maintains similar values and habits to them. The opposite should be our goal—mingle and associate with the lost but don't take on their values or habits. That way we, as both salt and light, have our proper effect of preserving and exposing in order to bring them into their destiny. Healthy families that are intentional breed healthy families.

One of our local high schools was having a problem with some of their students. Some parents had lost control of their kids and were clueless as to what to do. The school was considering removing these students permanently from their program. The principal recognized an unusual gift for family life in a couple of our pastors. Their heart was not to dominate or take over; they simply wanted to serve. The principal took a huge risk and asked them to come and mentor these parents about functional home life. The transformation within the families' relationships was amazing. Teenagers who had previously cursed their parents to their face were suggesting the whole family play a board game before they all went to bed. Some of them requested a regular time to talk each evening. The turnaround was so astonishing that there is a waiting list of public schools that want this team to come and work with their parents.

When parents have godly character and wisdom for raising children, they produce a family that reflects the love and integrity of Christ. If children grow up seeing one standard in church and another at home, they tend to rebel against standards altogether. Conversely, when integrity is genuine both in and out of the public eye, children grow up willing to pay the price needed to follow in their parents' footsteps, as long as they have been given room for individuality.

This is one area where an ounce of effort translates into a pound of impact. Few families actually purposely live the adventure of life together. Embracing such an adventure together is what gives place for creative expression to surface. My wife has been so good for our household in this area. She is adventurous by nature and tends to add joy to the things I might unintentionally crush by my intensity. I learned from her, because I wanted to learn. My family is better, and I am better, because of her quest for creativity in the home.

This simply means that we always do things to the best of our ability. Sometimes money is tight. Excellence can't be measured in buying the finest car or the most expensive clothes. Rather it is displayed in our approach to life—all of us, for all of Him. It's a great deal!

GOVERNMENT

Knowing that Jesus is the "desire of the nations" encourages us as we approach this mountain of influence. It means our simple task is to make the desired One visible.

Government usually lives in a crippled state because of the fear of voters. Noble people enter that world and end up losing their dreams on the altar of intimidation. The leaven of Herod poisons many (see Mark 8:15). But there is a new breed being groomed for this hour who fears only God and lives with a wisdom that enables one to dance through the minefield of public opinion. Such is the price of working effectively in government.

Those who climb this mountain of influence must realize that it is necessary to increase "in favor with God and men" (Luke 2:52), just as Jesus did. Proverbs is probably the most practical book of instruction on this subject. Reading a chapter a day, according to the date, will give leaders in this realm a compass bearing so that no issue arises that doesn't have a Kingdom solution.

One of the women in our congregation was recently working in an Arab country for the U.S. State Department. She was invited to give input into the educational system in that country. They had a problem with the discipline of high school boys, and though they rarely empower women in their country at that level, the favor upon her life was larger than the cultural barrier. She addressed the instructors and then wrote a paper on the subject, based on the principles we live by in our church—all Kingdom principles of discipline. Their educational leaders were so impressed with the report that they adopted it as the standard of discipline for their school system for the entire nation. The U.S. embassy responded in like manner, sending the report to their embassies around the world.

It is unfortunate that the words integrity and politician are considered an oxymoron. The Word of God remains true—"when it goes well with the righteous, the city rejoices" (Prov. 11:10). People instinctively want to be governed by people who are honest and righteous. They want leaders who are not self-serving, but who will actually govern sacrificially for the benefit of the whole. Here again is where we need to embrace the standard of Jesus, which is to serve like a king and rule like a servant. It is His way.

It is sad to see believers who fall to the political tactics of unbelieving opponents because their popularity has declined in the public opinion polls. There are better ways of doing things, from running a campaign to surrounding oneself with people of wisdom for good decisions. All of these things are marks of a person committed to the wisdom of creativity.

Two of the most basic roles of government are to create a realm of safety and a realm of prosperity. When governmental leaders use their position for personal gain, it amounts to prostituting their charisma for themselves. Excellence is found in doing our best for the sake of others.

SCIENCE & MEDICINE

This is becoming a bigger influence in the world all the time. Diseases are on the increase, with little sign of cures. I believe in divine healing and have seen thousands healed through Jesus Christ, but I'm not opposed to medical intervention. The entire medical community is gaining power, credibility, and influence throughout our society.

One of our ministry targets is to pray for all those who are with the dying. That includes doctors and nurses, ambulance workers, convalescent hospital employees, police, firefighters, and so on. We are praying that the righteous will be assigned to those places of influence, because we want to make it nearly impossible to get to hell from our city.

We have a person in a place of authority in one of the convalescent hospitals in our area. It is written on the medical charts that the nurses must call her when anyone is dying so she can be with them. If necessary she will even remove the family members from that patient for a few minutes while she prays with them to receive Christ. We don't want people politely going to hell from our city. You have heard the saying, *there are no atheists in foxholes*—the same could be said of those on the edge of eternity. People are very receptive to the Truth when they are facing death. Authentic love and compassion for people, expressed by those planted within that system, brings forth a wonderful harvest. It's amazing what we are allowed to do when we go in low just to serve. People know the difference between authentic love and a person fulfilling their religious obligations. Real love has very few opponents.

Christ-like character always puts others first. This highly respected industry has fallen on hard times due to the great number of doctors who make questionable decisions based on profit margins. Hospitals are often in the crosshairs of critics as they often operate without compassion. Yet that is not the norm. Most in this profession at least started out with sincere compassion and a desire to help others. Kingdom-oriented people will once again be easy to spot, as the need is so great. And if those individuals believe in the power of God to heal, all the better. Miracles occur through the hands of medical professionals at an increasing rate. The number of doctors who attend our healing conferences is growing dramatically. It's a beautiful combination when we see a whole segment of society raised up that can work in both the natural and the supernatural realms to bring about good health.

More and more Christian doctors are being trained by God to find answers to health issues. As wonderful as healing is, divine health is greater. Believers have been given access to the mysteries of the Kingdom regarding this subject. It would be tragic to come to the end of time and have the only generation to experience divine health be the Israelites. They lived under an inferior covenant and were in rebellion against God. Inferior covenants cannot make superior promises. Those in this mountain of influence have access to things that the entire world is aggressively asking for. Asking God for specific solutions will enable those involved in medicine to give true creative expression to a dying world.

This group of professionals has a head start in the area of excellence, as they are accustomed to paying a significant price for their role in society. If they can maintain passion and discipline, while embracing a humble heart, nothing will be impossible for them.

Passion for God Creates Passion for Other Things

Staying passionate and encouraged is vital while facing the privilege of ascending these mountains of influence. Passion wears out when it relies solely on self-motivation. God has fire in His eyes! Frequent encounters with Him will keep any flame in us burning. But encouragement is another matter. "One who speaks in a tongue edifies himself" (1 Cor. 14:4 NASB). Dr. Lance Wallnau adds an interesting twist to the word *edifies*. He points out that edifice is a related word, and that one who prays in tongues builds the edifice from which the purposes of God for their life becomes manifest! Perhaps this is why the apostle Paul claimed that he spoke in tongues more than anyone else. He was building something big for God!

Endnotes

1. A word of knowledge is when a person knows something about someone else that they couldn't know without God revealing it to them. In this case, Chad received a word of knowledge about specific illnesses that some of the shoppers had and that God wanted to heal them.

2. Involvement in the political process is not only acceptable for the believer, it is essential. We just cannot lower our standards by thinking that our strength is in the political process. Natural efforts in obedience to God bring spiritual release. His invasion is our strength.

HOW DO WE

TAKE OVER THE WORLD?

WE MUST HAVE A STRATEGY.

∽ 2 ∾

THE SEVEN MOUNTAIN MANDATE

Lance Wallnau

My first encounter with the revelation of the seven mountains of culture goes back to a conversation I had with Loren Cunningham in the year 2000. Loren is the esteemed founder of Youth With A Mission (YWAM), a global missionary organization with an emphasis on enlisting young people in the call to serve Jesus. He shared how, in 1975, he was praying about how to turn the world around for Jesus and saw seven areas. He said, "I saw that we were to focus on these categories to turn around nations to God. I wrote them down and stuck the paper in my pocket."

This was his list:

1. Church

2. Family

3. Education

4. Government and law

5. Media (television, radio, newspaper, Internet)

6. Arts, entertainment, sports

7. Commerce, science, and technology

The day after this revelation, he had a divine appointment. As he put it, "I met with a dear brother, Dr. Bill Bright, leader of Campus Crusade for Christ. He shared with me how God had given him a message, and he felt he needed to share it with me. God had identified areas to concentrate on to turn the nations back to Him! They were the same areas with different wording. Bill was stunned when I took the same notes out of my pocket and showed them to him."

As I heard Loren tell me this story, I was somewhat stunned. It seemed odd that this message had been out since 1974, yet I had not heard about it earlier. It so transformed my thinking that I have made it central to my message ever since. Loren called these seven areas "mind molders," and Bill Bright called them "world kingdoms." I saw them as seven mountains whose lofty heights are mind molders with strongholds that occupy influence as world kingdoms. Each of the seven mountains represents an individual sphere of influence that shapes the way people think. These mountains are crowned with high places that modern-day kings occupy as ideological strongholds. These strongholds are, in reality, houses built out of thoughts. These thought structures are fortified with spiritual reinforcement that shapes the culture and establishes the spiritual climate of each nation. I sensed the Lord telling me, "He who can take these mountains can take the harvest of nations."

Loren felt that the strategy to take the seven mountains would be very straightforward. In *Making Jesus Lord*, he writes:

> First, we take territory from satan in the place of prayer, with the power of the Holy Spirit, through the mighty weapons available to us. We know that spiritual warfare involves pulling down strongholds of false reasoning. We pray against the enemy's influence in whatever area we are aware. Our prayers should be specific. Listening to the Holy Spirit in our minds, He will tell us how to pray. Regional and local matters should be part of our specific focus.
>
> Second, after we have prayed for a specific sphere of influence, be it government, a school system, an area of the media, or whatever, God may then choose to use us in the very sphere for which we have been praying. He may call us to penetrate that influential place for Him, placing us, like Daniel or Joseph, in a place of authority.[1]

I agree with Loren that our strategy must include spiritual intervention from our position of authority within the Church, as well as influence from our position of authority in the marketplace. In order to take the seven mountains of culture for Christ's Kingdom, we must understand the interaction between the Church, the Gospel, and the culture. An idea I heard a few years ago clarifies this division. There are only four ways we can approach this mission:

1. The Church preaches the Gospel, but is separated from culture:
   Church + Gospel – Culture = Fundamentalism

2. The Church is gathering for social causes, but not preaching the Gospel:
   Church – Gospel + Culture = Liberalism

3. The Gospel is being preached and the culture embraced, but not by the Church:
   Gospel + Culture – Church = Para Church

4. All three are lined up:
   Church + Gospel + Culture = Kingdom

We really don't have a choice in the matter. Without all three—Church, Gospel, and culture—we will fail to change the world in any permanent way. It will require nothing less than the government of God to dispossess and occupy the territory dominated by the gates of hell. This is a supernatural commission that requires the Holy Spirit and spiritual authority to pull off. Some things can be done by casual fellowship, like sipping coffee at Starbucks, but this is not one of them. We need to see the words "...I will build My church, and the gates of Hades shall not prevail against it" (Matt. 16:18 NKJV) in a fresh light. The Church needs to expand its vision of what it takes to "make disciples of all the nations" (Matt. 28:19).

LOST GOSPEL, LOST KINGS

As part of my seven mountain journey, I interviewed a key Washington leader who is often referred to as the "stealth Billy Graham" because of his influence behind the scenes with leaders of nations and foreign governments. Out of respect for him, I will leave his name anonymous.

I had not even shaken his hand when he at once set me up with this question: "Who were the people groups God assigned to the apostle Paul? To whom was he sent to preach?"

My mind raced because I knew it was a trick question. If I say Jews, he may say Gentiles, I thought to myself, but if I say Gentiles, he may say Jews. Reminded of the prophet who said, "I have a word for someone in the room right now, and the Lord shows me that they are either a male or female," I said, "Both."

He said, "Wrong." Turning to Acts 9:15, he read to me the words spoken to Ananias as he reluctantly went to minister to the renowned persecutor, Saul of Tarsus: "Go, for he is a chosen vessel of Mine to bear My name before Gentiles, kings, and the children of Israel" (NKJV). He put his finger to my chest and uttered the unforgettable words: "Everyone forgets the kings!"

Who are the modern-day kings? They are the ones who occupy the high places, the spheres of influence in the seven mountains of culture. They write the songs you sing and make the movies you watch. They tell you what's in fashion and what's out. They design the iPhone and determine the price of gas. They craft the legislation you live with, and they send your sons to war. They straddle the thrones at the top of the seven mountains. Sociologists refer to them as remnant elites, but we might be more comfortable calling them gatekeepers. Simply stated, a mountain king is someone with a significant sphere of authority.

Every 7M (seven mountain) king has a position in a high place and influences their own sphere directly and other spheres indirectly. Kings do not have to be virtuous, but they do have to be competent or they won't last long because all kings know other kings who would like to take their thrones. This is not the culture of sheep; it is a culture more conducive to wolves. High places, the spheres of influence where kings position themselves, are the specific target and habitation of darkness. In fact, the apostle Paul revealed to the Ephesians that much of their wrestling was not with rulers made of flesh and blood, but rather against "spiritual hosts of wickedness in the heavenly places" (Eph. 6:12 NKJV).

How does hell ensure control of this strategic ground? The fact that high-level spiritual powers guard these realms is indicated in the temptation of Jesus in the wilderness. Satan showed the Prince of Glory all the kingdoms of the world and said, "All this authority I will give You, and their glory; for this has been delivered to me, and I give it to whomever I wish" (Luke 4:6 NKJV). Mountain kings wield incredible influence and power, and they need to hear the Gospel!

My Washington friend, having succeeded in besting me with the Pauline question, pointed out another verse to set me up for another question: "Look here, Lance, and notice where Jesus sent His disciples: 'Behold, I send you out as sheep in the midst of wolves…'" (Matt. 10:16 NKJV). My friend then posed this question: "To whom are they to go when they visit the wolf pack?"

I was stumped again and came up with the rather lame spiritual answer, "Wherever God leads them?"

My mentor was not fazed at discovering my labyrinth of ignorance. He turned to another verse, "Now whatever city or town you enter, inquire who in it is worthy, and stay there till you go out" (Matt. 10:11 NKJV).

No longer questioning me, he explained it this way:

> At first I thought Jesus was telling the disciples to go to the nicest rabbi in town and start there, but really, that would be hard to do outside of Israel, and certainly it would be hard to imagine worthy rabbis who were also wolves. Who was Jesus telling them to start with? They were to go first to the community member whom the people placed the highest value upon, the one with worth and influence. The Gospel of the Kingdom is a proclamation to these wolf packs of influential "mountain kings," that another King has arrived and that this King is unlike any other. He is the judge of all men, the

King over all kings. He is a good King and the
best friend that any wolf has ever had.

In fact, if the wolf will cooperate, he will find that the One King who rules over all men and judges nations will help that wolf king succeed. This all-powerful One will drive out the influence of the powers of "spiritual wickedness," that fester and thrive off of the chaos and control they exercise in that king's domain. When wolf kings honor the King of glory, they do not become weak kings. Quite the contrary, they become truly great, and more so, they have authority to reveal the glory hidden within their sphere of authority.

Is there indeed glory in the seven mountains of culture? During the wilderness temptation of Jesus:

> *The devil, taking Him up on a high mountain, showed Him all the kingdoms of the world in a moment of time. And the devil said to Him, "All this authority I will give You, and their glory; for this has been delivered to me, and I give it to whomever I wish"* (Luke 4:5-6 NKJV).

The kingdoms of this world were not created by the devil. In fact, he said, "All this has been delivered to me, and I give it to whomever I wish."

The kingdoms were made for humanity. These kingdoms possess the capacity to reveal the glory of the One who called them into being. In the last chapter of the Bible, when the will of God is fully manifest on earth as it is in Heaven, there will be a complete takeover of the earth. The kingdoms of this world will be the kingdoms of our Lord and of His Christ, and the great city of God will be doing heavenly business with kings of the earth: "And they shall bring the glory and the honor of the nations into it [the celestial city]" (Rev. 21:26 NKJV). Notice how certain things continue on into eternity—an accessible heavenly city and kings and nations on the earth! Especially notice that there is an inexhaustible supply of "glory and honor" hidden under the sphere of the kings in these nations.

Does the Kingdom Have a Church?

It seems clear that the Church has a Kingdom to proclaim, but does the Kingdom have a church? This came home to me in a powerful way in the year 2000 when I was invited to South Korea to train CEOs and executive coaches by my friend, Dr. Joseph Umidi, who was at that time a professor at Regent University. I remember doing some research before arriving and finding out that 50 of the largest churches in the world came out of South Korea. I thought that revealed something to me about the discipline and spirituality of the believers in the culture, and therefore, I asked these businessmen the question: "How many of the top 100 companies in the world are run by or owned by a South Korean?" They were silent. I repeated the question through my interpreter twice because I thought they did not understand.

Then a man stood reluctantly to his feet and made a remarkable disclosure. "Sir," he said rather timidly, "I am neither a CEO nor an executive coach. I am here today because I needed to sneak in as a businessman to hear you. I pastor a youth church in Seoul, Korea, and the Lord told me the future of our ministry was tied into the revelation you will preach." He came up to the board where I had illustrated the seven mountains and pointed to the church mountain saying, "We have taught our people how to build the Church, but we have not taught them how to take the Kingdom!" as he circled the other six mountains.

Joseph wisely suggested that I be still and just watch what would happen next. Another young man stood up and said he had a confession to make. He was tall, had a deep voice, and spoke English rather well. He explained that he had attended Parker Business School in the United States and was a successful electronics entrepreneur. He had, however, always felt a desire to be the president of South Korea. Up until that day, he was convinced that this was a selfish desire and that his best service was to contribute money to build the Church. But now he was publicly repenting of believing a lie. He realized that his political aspirations were not sinful after all.

The CEOs stood up next, but they did not rise to repent. They surrounded the young man in prayer and told him that, if he would do diligence and prepare himself as a qualified candidate, they would be honored to support his candidacy. It was a historic moment for me because I could see how quickly the Body of Christ can rise up with impact if the Kingdom is taught.

ALL THE MOUNTAINS BELONG IN THE KINGDOM

I think I was guilty at one time of doing the same thing to others that some well-meaning Christians did to that young man. When we think that the Church Mountain is the only spiritual mountain, we form a great divide between the Church and culture. We imply that the Church is the holy spiritual mountain and the rest of the mountains are of the world and profane.

The shocking truth is that each mountain is a spiritual mountain! The devil's skill in leading us to think differently has resulted in the spiritual invasion of foreign deities into every area once held by followers of Christ. As we surrendered our colleges and universities, the intellectual seducing spirits of false enlightenment took the hippies of the 1960s and made them the professors who teach your children in college today! This invasion is all the more ironic when you consider that the first 230 colleges and universities established in the United States were planted for the education and development of Christians, ministers in particular. This secular-sacred split has made the Church Mountain almost entirely irrelevant to society today.

The truth is that all nations are already being discipled through the belief systems of those occupying their high places, the peak institutions of a nation's mind molders. If the Church leaves a vacuum by failing to occupy these high places with the teaching of the Kingdom, the enemy will seek to disciple the nations by building strongholds of deception that are guarded and advanced through those decision makers who rise to the top of the seven mountains of culture.

Perhaps Jesus' description of the wheat and the tares makes more sense when seen in the light of our struggle in nations. The enemy had access to the harvest field to plant his corrupting seed "while men slept" (Matt. 13:25 NKJV). As long as the Church thinks the purpose of the Great Commission is anything less than penetrating and occupying the mind molders of the nations in order to bring about a sustained influence that shapes the culture, we are asleep. The fields, our nations, are not only vulnerable to the enemy, but they are also being aggressively cultivated right under our noses.

In the Old Testament, God warned Israel that if they did not drive out the inhabitants of the land, the very peoples with whom they compromised would come after them. These inhabitants would be "barbs in your eyes and thorns in your sides" (Num. 33:55 NIV 1984). The sober truth is that everywhere the Church fails to exercise her authority, a vacuum opens for darkness to occupy. By rejecting the culture, we reject our spiritual authority to influence that culture. In the last days, however, there is no neutral territory. What we don't possess becomes fair game to occupy for the purpose of harassing us!

TAKING THE SEVEN MOUNTAINS

Here are some salient points to keep in mind as we embrace the message of the seven mountains.

The business of shifting culture or transforming nations does not require a majority of conversions. We make a mistake when we focus on winning a harvest in order to shape a culture. Together, Protestants and Catholics make up a 70 percent majority of the U.S. population, and as such already have a majority consensus on key matters affecting marriage and abortion. Yet they are still incapable of being more than a firewall to the minority, who are advancing a same-sex ideology. If we do not need more conversions to shift a culture, what do we need? We need more disciples in the right places, the high places. Minorities of people can shape the agenda, if properly aligned and deployed. The greatest gains in gay rights occurred during 10 years of our most conservative presidencies, and their movement has never been larger than 5 to 6 percent of the population.

The Church lacks cultural power because it focuses on changing the world from within the Church Mountain rather than releasing the Church into the marketplace to leaven all seven mountains. The goal isn't to pull a convert out of the world and into a church, as we so often do. The goal is to be the Church that raises up disciples who go into all the world. Taking the Gospel into all the world is no longer a simple journey of geography. The world is a matrix of overlapping systems or spheres of influence. We are called to go into the entire matrix and invade every system with an influence that liberates that system's fullest potential.

Isaiah described this process:

*Now it shall come to pass in the latter days that
the mountain of the Lord's house shall be established on the top of the mountains, and shall be
exalted above the hills; and all nations shall flow
to it* (Isaiah 2:2 NKJV).

The command of Jesus to teach and "make disciples of all
the nations" (Matt. 28:19 NKJV) implies that there is a dis-
tinctly biblical way of thinking and seeing the world. You do
not need to know everything about every sphere, but you do
need to master your own sphere by seeking out the wisdom of
God—His way of thinking and seeing for that area. There is
wisdom for every sphere, be it economics, art, marriage, education, government, and so forth. Start by mastering the fun-
damentals and trust that God will advance you to His hidden
wisdom and revelation that, once applied, will produce superior results.

Each sphere has a unique structure, culture, and stronghold of thinking—a worldview of its own. The battle in each
sphere is over the ideas that dominate that sphere and between
the individuals who have the most power to advance those
ideas. The apostle Paul addressed this battle in his admonition
that we "do not wrestle against flesh and blood, but against
principalities, against powers..." (Eph. 6:12 NKJV). He tells us
that, in dealing with these strongholds of thinking, our battle
is in "casting down arguments and every high thing that exalts
itself against the knowledge of God" (2 Cor. 10:5 NKJV). The
Church must be represented in each sphere if the power of

darkness is to be broken. It is the Church alone that has spiritual authority to come against the gates of hell.

Those at the top of these spheres have the power to grant a person a sphere authority by simply inviting them into it. This is part of the blessing and power that comes when you allow your peace to rest upon those at the top of the mountain you are invited to. When Saul permitted David to slip into the role of a soldier for a moment, David slew a giant and gained permanent access to the government mountain (see 1 Sam. 17). When Paul, a political prisoner, healed an island chief's father after a shipwreck, he was given an immediate upgrade of authority on the island (see Acts 28:7-10).

We carry something as kings and priests that is powerful. It is, in fact, a combined anointing. As kings, we have authority to administrate over earth and all demonic opposition. As priests, we have power to access heavenly places in Christ. Combined together, our identity as kings and priests allows us to access the throne of Grace and receive not only strength but also instruction and divine blueprints that we then administrate on earth. We are salt. We slow down the decay of culture. We are also light, which means that we illuminate a pathway into a better future.

In fact, we who have tasted the powers of the age to come have authority to bring the power of that age into the present (see Heb. 6:5). As we do this, we access the power to manifest the testimony of Jesus. "This gospel of the kingdom will be preached in all the world as a witness to all the nations, and then the end will come" (Matt. 24:14 NKJV). We are to be witnesses who demonstrate evidence of the reality of the Kingdom.

The world needs our witness of His Kingdom. When we witness to His Kingdom, we are manifesting the testimony of Jesus. Our witness shows that He is who He said He is and that He can do what He said He can do! "Worship God! For the testimony of Jesus is the spirit of prophecy" (see Rev. 19:10 NKJV). To be light to the world is to reflect the illuminating power of the coming age right in the midst of this one. It is to see the future and bring it into the present so that others can know what the coming Kingdom looks like.

What will being light to the world look like? What does it mean for us to bring the future to the present and thus display the Kingdom of God to the world? God is waiting for us to access His presence, His counsel, and His insight so that we can apply Heaven's solutions to earth and teach His ways by demonstrating solutions to problems. What Jesus demonstrated in healing human bodies is the same power that can transform nations. The leaves of the tree of life have power to heal nations! We have access to something that can fix broken systems among the nations. We have authority to heal sick systems in the seven mountains of culture. The following are the seven mountains and the maladies that humanity creates without someone to proclaim the truth and make crooked things straight:

Religion: People suffer from broken fellowship with God.

Families: Wounded fathers and mothers break from each other in divorce, and their children—often unprotected—experience exploitation, abuse, and abandonment.

Education: Broken systems in the United States fail to educate students, and illiteracy causes over half of the world to miss out on the promise of prosperity.

Government: Broken systems of justice, destructive legislation, and corruption plague entire regions of the earth.

Media and Arts: Broken oracles that do not speak the truth produce defiled images and destructive sounds and twist the image of what was made beautiful.

Science and Technology: Broken remedies and perverted science wreak global destruction.

Business: Broken economies, robbed of opportunities and dignity, are full of greed and poverty.

These are the high places we have left for the devil to dominate because we have failed to see our role as healers and deliverers. This is why Jesus said, "This gospel of the kingdom [not this Gospel of salvation] will be preached in all the world as a witness to all the nations" (Matt. 24:14 NKJV). A witness does not guarantee the jury will decide in your favor, but it does mean that nations will be without excuse if they choose to follow another way. Those who are anti-Christ will be so because they reject the testimony of Jesus Christ.

Right now the only testimony we seem to be offering is through the Church Mountain, as we proclaim the way of salvation and, perhaps, pray for a healing or word that endorses the supernatural authority of our message. Can you see how shallow our witness is when we refuse to make relevant the mighty power of Jesus over all things? We must not just limit His power to those things pertaining to the life to come.

The Holy Nation Living Out the Kingdom

Dr. Henry Kissinger opens the first paragraph of his best-selling book on diplomacy in the most interesting language. In describing the flow of history, he leads into the emergence of the United States in its role over the last 100 years:

> Almost as if according to some natural law, in every century there seems to emerge a country with the power, the will, and the intellectual and moral impetus to shape the entire international system in accordance with its own values.[2]

A secular historian like Kissinger cannot see the invisible cosmic struggle of principalities and powers that worked through demonized world rulers like Hitler, Stalin, or Mao, but he can see the aftermath in the formation of nations as the spoils of wars and upheavals. He is most certainly not trying to describe the role of the Church, but I think he defined a valid pattern in history that is setting things up for our role in this pivotal hour "as if according to some natural law, in every century there seems to emerge a country with the power… the moral impetus to shape the entire international system." I believe that we are now that nation that seeks to emerge, the holy nation of Jesus-followers, the Church. We have been given heavenly authority and power in this final hour to impact the earth with our King's values—the message of His Kingdom.

The Church is one holy or set apart nation in the midst of a multitude of nations. If what I am teaching is correct, all believers can become deliverers who arise like Joseph or Esther to save their nations and preserve the heritage of faith in their communities. You, more than any other person who does not know God, are uniquely called out from among others in your nation to be a citizen of Heaven with authority to bring Heaven and its unique resources and solutions into the earth. You can do this through the power of the Holy Spirit made manifest in your specific calling and assignment!

You are called to show forth the "praises" (the word here really can be interpreted as "the excellence") of Him who called you out of darkness (see 1 Pet. 2:9). You are called to enter into and engage in every earthly sphere of this world with a super- natural ability to manifest what God's Kingdom looks like. You are uniquely qualified to solve problems nobody else can solve!

When you do so, you "show forth the excellence of Him" and build a platform of profound credibility from which you can teach others His ways.

We are entering a bigger battle than most of us appreciate. Something is emerging in the earth that seeks to rob nations of their ability to stand up in the freedom of their unique autonomy and reveal the glory God has deposited in them. God loves the idea of nations, and nations are designed to reveal His glory. They are His special interest. What does it look like when the will of God is done on earth as it is in Heaven? Look at Revelation 21:24-26 and you see it! The kings of the earth are ruling over nations! They exist in eternity. What do those kings do? They cultivate the potential in those nations to glorify God! "They shall bring the glory and the honor of the nations" into the city of God and display the beauty of what God has placed in the nations (Rev. 21:26). Jesus intends that you and I, as modern-day kings and priests, teach nations His wonderful secrets. We are to make disciples, not of people only, but of nations.

None of this will be easy, which is why it is important to find your own company of like-minded believers whom you can stand with. If as believers we fail to do this, we will surrender power to an increasingly hostile devil who knows that he has but a short time. Remembering that the Kingdom of Heaven suffers violence, it is important to note that we are engaged in a real war (see 2 Cor. 10:2-6). You are about to pioneer the last great chapter of the journey of the Church into the Kingdom Age. It does not matter how large the obstacles are or how slender your present resources may appear to be. Jesus is once again telling His closest followers: "Do not fear, little flock, for it is your Father's good pleasure to give you the kingdom!" (Luke 12:32 NKJV).

ENDNOTES

1. Loren Cunningham and Janice Rogers, *Making Jesus Lord* (Seattle, WA: YWAM Publishing, 1988), 134-135.

2. Henry Kissinger, *Diplomacy* (New York: Simon & Schuster, 1994), 17.

CULTURAL TRANSFORMATION
CAN ONLY COME ABOUT
BY STRATEGIC PRAYER AND
SPIRITUAL WARFARE. THIS
KIND CAN COME OUT BY
NOTHING BUT PRAYER AND
FASTING (MARK 9:29).

≈ 3 ≈

OCCUPYING THE GATES OF THE HEAVENLY CITY

Alan Vincent

It is important to look at what the gates of a city allegorically represent. This was powerfully illustrated in the days of David's kingdom and again in the restored city of Jerusalem when it was rebuilt in the days of Nehemiah.

THE GATES BECOME SPIRITUAL

When we come to the books of the prophets and to some other Old Testament Scriptures, we find gates being spoken of prophetically; they are seen by the prophets to be spiritual, in the heavens, and not physical, on earth.

When we then go to the New Testament, we also find Jesus speaking allegorically of gates. Let us now look at what gates mean in terms of a strategy for establishing the Kingdom of God in our cities today.

The first thing that Jesus said about the Church He would build was that the "gates of Hades shall not prevail against it" (Matt. 16:18 NKJV). These gates came to represent the demonic spiritual powers that ruled over the cities from the heavenly realm. Those powers, through their various human agencies, regulated all that was allowed to come into the city spiritually, and they also controlled what was permitted to take place legally and politically in the city. Today, in many nations, these spiritual powers control many of the pillars of our society and our secular laws to such a degree that these spirits now rule the lives of the people in our cities. As I write, most of the spiritual gates over our cities are occupied by demonic powers working through their human agencies and not by God's people.

Long ago, satan took control of these gates in order to dominate our cities for his purposes. His occupancy in most cases is almost total. From these spiritual gates in the heavenly places, the influence of hell is much greater than the influence of Heaven; this is true for the majority of our cities.

This is how Jerusalem was controlled during the days of Jesus' ministry on earth. Demonic powers, working through the religious and political leaders of the day—such as the San-hedrin, Herod, and Pilate—were able to significantly limit the ministry of Jesus and His impact upon the city. Jesus knew that until He rose triumphantly from the dead, with all power and authority in Heaven and earth in His hands, these demonic powers could not be cast down. After Jesus had risen, however, and the Holy Spirit had fallen on the disciples on the Day of Pentecost, everything changed. The disciples quickly learned how to cast down the spirit powers over the city of Jerusalem.

Therefore, in order for the Kingdom to come to our cities in the same Pentecostal power of the first century Church, we must learn to retake these gates out of the enemy's hands and cast down these ruling spirits.

In Scripture, God has given us great promises concerning these gates. In Genesis 22, God spoke to Abraham after he had offered his only son, Isaac, and said:

> *Indeed I will greatly bless you, and I will greatly*
> *multiply your seed as the stars of the heavens*
> *and as the sand which is on the seashore; and*
> *your seed shall possess the gate of their enemies.*
> *In your seed all the nations of the earth shall*
> *be blessed, because you have obeyed My voice*
> (Genesis 22:17-18 NASB).

God promised Abraham that the true descendants of Abraham would, by faith, possess the gates of their enemies, resulting in the reaping of a mighty harvest.

In Genesis 24 we have a beautiful allegory of Christ and His Church. Isaac is the bridegroom representing Christ, and Rebekah is the bride representing the Church. Rebekah's relatives are about to send her away to be married to Isaac. In verse 60 God declares a promise to the bride, Rebekah, and allegorically to the Church:

> *They blessed Rebekah and said to her: "Our sis-*
> *ter, may you become the mother of thousands of*

> ten thousands; and may your descendants pos-
> sess the gates of those who hate them" (Genesis
> 24:60 NKJV).

The promise of reaping a mighty harvest is directly linked with taking possession of the gates that are presently in the hands of our enemy. Gate-taking was and still is a necessary preparation for city-taking. Also, once these gates are retaken, the spiritual blindness affecting the minds of many people will be immediately removed—and then the harvest can be reaped.

PHYSICAL GATES DIFFER FROM SPIRITUAL GATES

I do not believe it is enough to physically drive around a city and focus only on the major highways and other main entry points leading in and out of it. This can sometimes be the right thing to do, providing we have definitely heard from God and have some good spiritual reason for focusing in this way, but we cannot make it an automatic methodology.

We must only do this when God has specifically shown us first that these locations are spiritual strongholds or gates "erected" through some present or historical situation, and second, that they need to be taken back.

The gates that Jesus and the prophets referred to were not that kind of physical gate. Rather, they were spheres of influence and control emanating from the heavens that shaped the way the people of the city thought and behaved. They also controlled many of the civil laws and judicial decisions that were made to govern them. For clarity, let me now divide these spiritual "gates" into three categories.

Category #1: Gates That Control People's Thinking

These gates are largely responsible for shaping the worldview of most people. They influence people's minds and strongly formulate the way people think and behave. Several Scriptures tell us that we are fighting a battle for the minds of men, women, and especially children. The apostle Paul explains this truth in Second Corinthians 4:4:

> *Whose minds the god of this age has blinded, who do not believe, lest the light of the gospel of the glory of Christ, who is the image of God, should shine on them.*

Within this category of mind-influencing gates are several subcategories; let me define them as follows:

1) The Media

The media, including radio, television, movies, the Internet, iPods and other devices, DVDs, magazines, newspapers, and so forth, powerfully influences the way most people think. These gates largely shape worldviews.

2) The Education System

The present system of education is based in totally secular, humanistic, evolutionary philosophies that are often reinforced by atheistic or polytheistic worldviews. This system has, to a great extent, shaped the minds and perspectives of almost all of us from our earliest school days.

3) Various Religious Systems
Making Significant Inroads in Our Cities

Ancient pagan religions, such as those practiced by Aztecs and druids, and Hinduism, Buddhism, Confucianism, and Islam are resurging as influential in America. These belief systems are being widely taught, practiced, and tolerated in the United States and throughout the world. In addition, many of the traditional Christian denominations have fallen away and developed religious systems that are far removed from God and the truths of Scripture and are syncretistic and humanistic in their teaching and philosophy. There are also a number of more recent cults, some of which claim to be "Christian," but are teaching false doctrines; others are unashamedly pagan, occult, and anti-Christian.

4) The Political System and
Institutions of Government

If you read any honest history book about the United States, it is obvious that the majority of the founding fathers of the United States of America were God-fearing men with high standards of integrity and morality. Most of them were bold Christians who were also men of prayer. They openly prayed, individually and corporately, for God's wisdom for the

Constitution they were writing and the political structure they were forming. The Constitution was written based on these values.

These men, and often their families, came largely from European nations controlled by corrupt religious systems that worked in partnership with equally corrupt political systems. Together, these systems dominated the lives of ordinary people and exploited them financially and in every other way. Therefore, our Founding Fathers were determined to maintain freedom from any such system in America's newly formed government.

This resulted in the now famous First Amendment, which prohibited the making of any law respecting the establishment of religion. This has been interpreted by some as a "separation of church and state," although those words were never actually used in the Constitution. The Founding Fathers neither intended there to be any separation between the one true God and the State, nor was there any confusion as to who that God was. To them, He was the God and Father of our Lord Jesus Christ.

If we were to turn our attention to other nations of the world, we would have to write another whole book to document the widespread corruption, greed, and lack of honesty, integrity, and morality in almost every present political system ruling those nations. There are one or two exceptions, but of the present 192 members of the United Nations, you could probably count on the fingers of one hand only a few truly upright moral leaders and governments.

5) The Legal System and Institutions of Law

The original standards of integrity and impartiality for the federal and local judges of the United States, including even the Supreme Court, have been seriously eroded in recent years. Most judges unashamedly exhibit a strong political or moral bias in the judgments they bring. In addition, generally speaking, the attorneys who plead in these courts are not really concerned that justice be done, but rather with winning their case by any "legal" means so as to make money for themselves and for their clients.

6) Financial Institutions and Financial Systems

To our horror, many of us have recently discovered the depths of depravity that exist in the people and financial institutions we trusted. These "pillars" of our society and economy have suddenly been exposed, and some have collapsed in ruins. As a result, millions of workers and other innocent victims have lost their means of livelihood.

The shock waves of this debacle have reverberated around the world to affect almost every nation. Our own economy in the U.S. has been shaken to the core. Political leaders and economic experts rush around trying to salvage what they can and fix the enormous problems confronting us. The most disturbing feature of all this is that no one seems to be facing the real issue that caused of all this to happen, namely the insatiable greed and moral corruption in those who led these institutions. Until there is real repentance over these issues, and a return to God-fearing righteousness, we will not find any real solutions.

John Wesley lived in similar times during which terrible moral corruption was exposed in government, banking, and official religious circles. The greatest investment scandal in history called The South Sea Bubble had just burst and devastated the economy of Britain and had seriously affected the United States and a number of other nations.

John Wesley frequently spoke a famous maxim in that time of spiritual revival in Great Britain: "Having, first, gained all you can and, secondly saved all you can, then give all you can!"[1] His words produced a tremendously positive surge in the economy that particularly benefited the lower-paid workers, many of whom had formerly been unemployed. His maxim needs to be rediscovered and practiced by everyone today.

7) Cultural Traditions of the City and the Nation

Some national cultures are so invaded by demonic powers that the norms of acceptable social behavior bear down heavily on all of society. Many true Christians buckle under the strain and live compromised lives in that stifling atmosphere. Once again, we see the same pressures affecting the way we live— and we must not give in to them.

Paul, Peter, and James mention several times in Scripture the issues of speaking the truth, keeping our word, fulfilling our promises, paying our taxes honestly, and living as law-abiding citizens.

These words of Scripture were written to Christians living in a pagan Roman society for which such godly cultural norms were nonexistent. Roman culture was also a very chauvinistic society with a low regard for women. Yet, from the beginning, the Church lived God's way and not according to pagan Roman culture. In a short time, they began changing their society for the better. We see ungodly norms in a number of cultures today. We must not yield to them, even if we originate from one of those cultures.

We have much work to do. As you look at this list, tell me honestly from your own observation in this present time: How many of these "gates" are strongly influenced by the devil, and how many are powerfully influenced by the clear proclamation of the Kingdom of God by the true Church? I'm sure you would agree that in most cases these gates are almost totally in the control of the evil one. This tells us who is really running our cities and controlling our societies. It's time to change things; God is sending His Holy Spirit and empowering us to do just that!

This is a battle for the minds of people. As we read earlier, the Bible says that, "the god of this world has blinded the minds of the unbelieving…" (2 Cor. 4:4 NASB).

But it also tells us that, "it is the God who commanded light to shine out of darkness, who has shone in our hearts to give the light of the knowledge of the glory of God in the face of Jesus Christ" (2 Cor. 4:6 NKJV). He has also given us mighty and powerful weapons that are able to destroy everything that exalts itself against the knowledge of God (see 2 Cor. 10:4-5).

This is a fight that requires greater passion to win.

How much of what our children are learning in secular public schools makes them run after Jesus? How much of what they learn makes them run after the world and devilish things? How would you rate our universities in their desire or ability to lead students to seek after God? How about the media? If you're thinking like I am, you're saying, "Man, we have some work to do around here!"

We must take back the gates! The first way they can be taken is by praying for the people who already hold positions of great influence in these various realms. We must pray that they might be converted, or at least that their hearts are turned toward the Lord with a new godly fear.

There is no evidence that Nebuchadnezzar or Cyrus or Darius II were ever truly converted, but their hearts were definitely turned to have a healthy fear of the Lord God of Israel and a great respect for those who served Him. It would have been even better if they had been clearly and truly converted, but even so, they were moved by the prayers of God's intercessors to serve the Lord's purposes and cause His will to be done on earth.

The second way to take these gates is for Christians to actually occupy these places and positions and become God's salt in that situation. They must be unashamed and courageous, yet wise witnesses who are powerful in prayer. It is no good to gain a position, remain quiet, and hope to have an indirect influence on the world around you.

Look at how Joseph always boldly and publicly recognized his God as the source of the great wisdom he exhibited. As an open worshiper of Jehovah, he was appointed to a political position second only to Pharaoh in the whole Egyptian Empire.

Also, look at the way Daniel behaved. He was in a secular government position all his life. He was a powerful political figure, second only to the various pagan kings whom he served. But he made it clear to each one of them that his prophetic wisdom and insight came directly from the God who was Jehovah, the God of the Jews, the only true God.

Neither of these men would be quiet about the Person and the Power who enabled them to be who they were and do what they did. They made it very clear that what they did with such wisdom and authority happened only because of the awesome God they served. At the risk of their lives, they would neither keep quiet about their God, nor would they lower their moral and ethical standards to keep out of trouble. Instead, they were able to change their secular demonic environments so that God was honored, revered, and finally obeyed. They changed the entire political atmosphere of nations.

We need to pray for Christians in these high positions in our nations so that they may have the same boldness, take the same uncompromising stand, and have the same influence on all they serve or rule.

Category #2: Gates Where Demons Are Venerated and Worshiped

These are geographical sites of intense demonic strength and activity, such as temples, grottos, historic monuments, and worship sites where so-called "holy" objects, idols, and false gods were or still are being actively worshiped.

This includes shrines devoted to pagan gods or spirits, as well as places where statues of Mary, the Black Madonna, Baby Jesus, other "saints," or holy relics are venerated. It includes all the idols and religious objects of apostate Christianity and all the buildings, historic sites, and monuments of other religions and their false gods.

These gates would further include sites of witchcraft, especially places where witches, wizards, and warlocks gather, and shrines of demonic worship, especially places of present or past blood sacrifice, particularly human blood sacrifice.

In addition, sites where blood has been violently spilled, such as battle and massacre sites (particularly where vengeance was the motive of the massacre), can be powerful demonic gates. Other gates and areas include sites of sexual immorality, such as brothels or sex shops, and murder sites, such as abortion clinics.

These gates can only be taken by experienced, strong intercessors who know what they are doing and are truly being led by the Lord. It is usually necessary to go physically to those sites several times, sometimes over a prolonged period of time. In these situations, prayers that are Spirit-led and targeted by revelation of the Word must earnestly continue for a period of time. Sometimes praying right through the night as God directs is particularly effective. This is partly because so much demonic activity and witchcraft goes on under the cover of darkness.

God may direct the prayer team to perform certain specific prophetic acts. Prayers must be spoken in faith when and as God commands so as to tell the demons to leave, just as John did in the temple of Diana in Ephesus.[2]

Then they will have to obey. It's not how much noise you make, but the faith and authority by which you speak. All this must be done, not as a learned methodology, but only as God specifically directs and empowers His saints in a unique way in that particular situation and in His timing. Paul encountered Diana in Ephesus, but he didn't go into the temple or address her directly because the Lord did not give him that assignment. Intercessors must hear clearly from the Lord and know His timing when addressing these demonically controlled gates.

Once such a site has been cleansed, wherever possible, it needs to be permanently taken over by the saints and turned into a holy place of God's presence and peace.

Sometimes we have to learn how to go to such places in the Spirit because going there physically is impossible. It may be a private site within a city where we are not permitted to go, or it may be a closed country where Christians are not permitted. But there are no barriers in the spirit realm, and God is beginning to teach us how to move and go in the Spirit to places where we cannot go openly and physically. This all has to be done as God specifically directs.

Category #3: Gates in Individuals Possessed by Major Demonic Principalities

These instances involve people who have deliberately given themselves to serve satan directly because of the power, prominence, and material benefits they obtain from him. But there is always a price that they have to pay. Satan is a hard taskmaster, even to his own.

When a major demonic principality has entered and now controls a person, it works through that person to control many other people. Sometimes one spirit in one person can strongly influence the behavior of hundreds of thousands of people throughout a whole nation or even several nations. In this way, these spirits are able to affect great portions of the earth. Recent historical and political examples would be Napoleon, Adolph Hitler, Joseph Stalin, Mussolini, or General Franco. A present-day religious example would be the Dalai Lama and the tens of thousands who attend his Mandala-making ceremonies in various locations as he travels worldwide.

There are others we could name who are presently active in various parts of the world today, including some within the United States. We must not be ignorant of these forces at work to control cities, regions, and the world. Some people are caught up in passionately giving themselves to what appears to be a great cause and don't realize the demonic impartation that accompanies their interaction.

A great biblical example of this kind of person was the zealous, fanatical, demonized Pharisee called Saul. Before his conversion, he rampaged through three nations persecuting and killing Christians, throwing many into prison, and inspiring many thousands of Jews to hate Christians, attack them, and even kill them. The spirit in this one man powerfully influenced thousands of people in three nations to behave like him and viciously persecute untold numbers of believers, even to death.

The first apostles knew this human, demonically controlled gate. They stayed together in prayer in Jerusalem and refused to leave or be separated at the height of the persecution. Although the Scriptures do not actually record why the apostles stayed together, I believe from my own experience that the Spirit of God called the apostles to an emergency, powerful upper room prayer meeting to take this "gate" known as Saul. They prayed for the demon to be cast out of him. These prayers, plus the dying prayers of Jesus and Stephen, as Saul actively participated in each of their deaths, pricked his conscience deeply (see Luke 23:34; Acts 7:60).

As a result, Saul was suddenly and dramatically converted when he had a supernatural encounter with the risen Lord Jesus on the road to Damascus (see Acts 9). He was saved, delivered, and turned around on the spot to become one of the mightiest apostles of the early Church.

When this one man was converted and that gate was taken, the demonic activity of thousands of people, which in turn had caused the persecution of many Christians, suddenly ceased. The Christian Church in the three regions of Judea, Galilee, and Samaria suddenly had rest and were comforted, and the believers were greatly multiplied (see Acts 9:1-31).

There is a city named Kiambu in Kenya, which was described in a Transformations video produced by George Otis, Jr. of The Sentinel Group.[3] In this city all kinds of sin, immorality, crime, and witchcraft were going on, and no church could be successfully planted there. When a man of God went to that city, God showed him to pray until he found the gate that was causing all this. He was led to a particular shop in the High Street where a well-known witch ran a handicrafts and palmistry business. He was led to target that store and pray that the witch, along with her controlling demonic spirit, would leave town. Although she and her family had lived there for several generations, he prayed passionately for some time. One day she suddenly packed all her things and was gone.

The atmosphere of the entire city changed. This Christian man then started a church and began to evangelize. He soon had a church of about 2,000 people. Crime plummeted, sin and immorality almost disappeared from the city, and everything changed.

We need to target with our prayers those people who presently serve as "gates of satan." We must get to know them by name and find out where they meet, where they go, and what they do. I am talking about ardent anti-Christian secularists, sexually perverse activists, militant atheists, witches and warlocks, the passionate promoters of New Age, the devotees of Mother Earth, and other such nonbelievers. We must pray for them with love, not hate; but we must be firm, so that they might have their eyes opened. Then they can repent and be converted, and the demons will leave them. Otherwise, if they stubbornly persist in their cooperation with these spirits and their resistance to God, then it may become necessary to pray that God will take them out one way or another. But this kind of warfare must only be done as a result of an express, specific Word from God.

This type of "gate" also includes strong activists who are demonically empowered to passionately promote political causes like abortion, homosexuality, lesbian and gay rights, the ACLU, and militant atheism. They may also promote false religions such as Wicca and secret societies like Freemasonry, Mormonism, various false cults, subtle religious deceptions, demon-based martial arts, and other such things. They are sometimes violent fanatics of another religion.

We may hate what they do, but we must not hate them as individuals. The Bible teaches that we do not wrestle against flesh and blood, but against principalities and powers and the spiritual wickedness in heavenly places that control them (see Eph. 6:12). We need to pray for their deliverance from these demonic influences and for their conversion to Jesus so that God can turn them around, just as He did the apostle Paul. When Jesus possesses these gates, and these individuals become ardent promoters of the Kingdom of God, a tremendous shift occurs in the spirit realm.

We must use our heavenly authority to ensure that these demons are dethroned. Either the demons leave the person and the person gets saved; or if the person won't let them go, then the person and the demons in them must leave together. Either way, they have to go! When this actually takes place, the demonic canopy of darkness over a city or a region is removed and replaced by the canopy of the Kingdom of Heaven. Then everything changes for the better, and a great harvest can be reaped.

By the power of the blood Jesus shed on Calvary and by His resurrection, we have the authority and power to take back what satan has stolen from the Body of Christ. We are living in a critical time in history for the Church. It is time to take control of the gates of our minds and how we think. We must cleanse geographical regions that have been used for demonic worship and overthrow the spiritual powers that have hindered the growth and fullness of the Kingdom of God on earth. It is an exciting time to be alive, and we certainly have much work to do!

Endnotes

1. Albert Outler, *John Wesley's Sermons: An Anthology* (Abingdon Press, October 1991), 355.

2. Ramsay MacMullen, *Christianizing the Roman Empire (A.D. 100-400)* (New Haven, CT: Yale University Press, 1984), 26.

3. George Otis Jr, *Transformations*, video (Sentinel Group, 1999).

We need divine strategies to infiltrate the systems of the world and to effectively work within them. Once the spiritual gates have opened to us, we need great wisdom to steward and distribute the resources God funnels our way.

⪦ 4 ⪧

STEWARDING FOR REFORMATION

C. Peter Wagner

The question in the minds of many who are bold enough to probe beneath the surface is: Why haven't we seen more of the reformation that we've been talking about? In my personal reckoning, the season in which those of us who are charismatically inclined evangelicals began to put the Dominion Mandate front and center began in 1990, and it sharply accelerated after the turn of the century. We have been doing everything we know how to do to see our cities transformed. However, after 20 years we cannot point to a single city in America that has been reformed according to objective sociological measurements.

Yes, we have recorded and circulated encouraging anecdotes. There are many tangible signs that God is powerfully at work. Prayers have been answered, many of them dramatically. Prophecies have been fulfilled, some with extraordinary accuracy. Public officials have been converted and have dedicated their jurisdictions to God. Food supplies are reaching the hungry. Crime rates have dipped in a number of places. Proposition 8, defining marriage as a one-man, one-woman union, was victorious in the 2008 general election in California. New polls show that the majority of Americans are pro-life. We are praying harder than ever. We are worshiping more intensely. We have a record-breaking number of mega-churches in the United States. And I could go on.

But the frustration persists. Reformation seems more elusive than we expected. Thoughtful people will naturally ask why. Are we doing something wrong? Is something missing? What changes do we need to make?

There are certainly many answers to these questions. The particular missing piece that I want to address in this chapter is money. I repeat, *money*! Trust me. We will not see measureable, sustained transformation of our cities or states or nations if those who are providing strategic leadership do not have access to large sums of money. Throughout human history, three things have contributed toward the reformation of society more than anything else, namely, violence, knowledge, and wealth. And the greatest of these is wealth!

The Spirit of Poverty

This has not been a very popular concept in the Religion Mountain. Of all the seven mountains, the Religion Mountain typically has the most negative views of wealth. Why is this? I believe it is due largely to the pervasive influence that the spirit of poverty has been able to gain in the Religion Mountain.

Just a glance at Deuteronomy 28, for example, will quickly convince you that God's desire for His people is for them to prosper. The first half of Deuteronomy 28 lists the abundant blessings that God showers on those who obey Him, and the second half lists the curses that await those who disobey Him. Prosperity is the will of God, while poverty is the will of satan. The spirit of poverty is satan's agent assigned to infiltrate the Church with the pervasive notion that there is something very suspicious about prosperity. It made great strides in the Middle Ages when monks were required to take a vow of poverty. Since they were considered to be the most spiritual individuals in the community, the idea that poverty must be a sign of piety took root, and unfortunately, it persists throughout much of the Religion Mountain today.

I would go so far as to say that we will not experience sustained social reformation unless and until we successfully bind the spirit of poverty through the blood of Jesus Christ and command it to loose its hold on the people of God. I believe that we need to come against this spirit of darkness by moving in the opposite spirit, which is the spirit of prosperity. It is wrong and even selfish to expect God to provide only "sufficiency" because mere sufficiency does not allow you to supply funding for God's causes—you need to spend all you have on yourself. No, believers should learn how to enjoy prosperity without succumbing to greed or covetousness or above all to mammon, an equally pernicious agent of darkness. Godly prosperity, then, will provide surplus wealth available for advancing the Kingdom of God.

THE DOMINION MANDATE

Let's think about advancing the Kingdom of God. Jesus taught us to pray, "Your kingdom come. Your will be done on earth as it is in heaven" (Matt. 6:10). All we need to do is go back to Genesis chapter 1 to be reminded of God's original purpose for creation. After creating everything else in five days, He created humans on the sixth. He told them to be fruitful and multiply and fill the earth, and then He informed them that they were supposed to take dominion over what He had just created (see Gen. 1:28). Although this was God's plan, it was hijacked by satan's success in tempting Adam and Eve to disobey God. The result was that satan usurped the authority that Adam was supposed to have over the creation and went on to become the god of this age and the prince of the power of the air (see Eph. 6:12).

Satan virtually had his way over the human race until Jesus came. Jesus was called the "last Adam" because, through His death and resurrection, He turned things back around (see 1 Cor. 15:20-28, 45). He came to seek and to save that which was lost. What was lost? The dominion over creation was lost because Adam forfeited it in the Garden of Eden. Jesus brought a new Kingdom, the Kingdom of God, which was to replace the perverse kingdom that satan had established. He came to reconcile the world back to Himself, and

He assigned the ministry of reconciliation to us (see 2 Cor. 5:18). Since then, it has been the responsibility of the people of God, empowered by the Holy Spirit, to regain the dominion that Adam was originally supposed to have. This is the Dominion Mandate.

Take, for instance, Jesus' Great Commission: "Go therefore and make disciples of all the nations…" (Matt. 28:19 NKJV). Previously many of us interpreted that to mean that we were to go into the nations in order to win as many souls as possible. Now, in light of the Dominion Mandate, we take it literally and see that we are to disciple nations as whole social units. Our task, then, is nothing less than reforming nations or people groups or social units of whatever scope. The values and blessings of God's Kingdom must become characteristic of whole cities or states or countries. But practically speaking, part of the process of making that happen is to have large amounts of wealth available.

By way of example, many of us who are advocating social change are fond of pointing out that it does not necessarily require a majority to bring it about. A favorite, albeit tragic, illustration relates to the gay agenda in the U.S. Even though the homosexual population of our nation is very small as a percentage, a concerted effort on their part has succeeded in altering the social psychology of our country. Homosexuality is now gaining the status of an acceptable form of sexual orientation, and state after state is legitimizing gay marriage. How can such a fractional minority accomplish such a lofty goal? Obviously it is because their leadership was able to forge a brilliant strategy designed to penetrate all seven mountains, but the strategy itself, in all likelihood, would not have succeeded were it not for massive funding. I subscribe to The Chronicle of Philanthropy, and I stand amazed (as well as appalled!) at the huge quantity of grant money directed to gay causes across our nation!

It is no wonder that Solomon said, "...Money answers everything" (Eccl. 10:19). In light of this, we must take the steps necessary to see that wealth pours into the hands of Kingdom-minded and Kingdom-motivated leaders who can successfully move God's people into sustained reformation of society. This is the will of God. The Bible says, "Your gates shall be open continually; they shall not be shut day or night, that men may bring you the wealth of the Gentiles..." (Isa. 60:11 NKJV).

The Great Transfer of Wealth

A great transfer of wealth from the unrighteous to the righteous is imminent. The assurance of this has come through a number of recognized prophets who are hearing from the Holy Spirit. I have learned to listen carefully to the prophets because the Bible says, "Surely the Lord God does nothing, unless He reveals His secret to His servants the prophets" (Amos 3:7). These prophecies began in the early 1990s, and they have continued. There have been a few promising signs, such as donations of $1.5 billion to the Salvation Army and $50 million to Wycliffe Bible Translators and $30 million to Young Life, but much more is to come. Why has it been delayed for almost 20 years?

The answer to this must have to do with God's timing. The wealth is undoubtedly there, but apparently we are not yet ready to receive it. For one thing, I believe that God was waiting for the biblical government of the Church to come into place under apostles and prophets. But this happened in 2001 when, at least according to my estimates, the Second Apostolic Age began. What more? I now think that in order for us to be able to handle the wealth responsibly, we need to recognize, identify, affirm, and encourage the ministry of apostles in the six non-religion mountains. They may or may not want to use the term "apostle," but they will function in Kingdom-based leadership roles characterized by supernaturally empowered wisdom and authority. We have more work to do here.

INFRASTRUCTURE DESIGN

Meanwhile, God has given us a design for an infrastructure that can handle any quantity of Kingdom wealth responsibly. It begins with the four links in the chain of wealth transfer:

THE FOUR LINKS

PROVIDERS   MANAGERS   DISTRIBUTORS   FIELD MARSHALS

As you can see, the links are Providers, Managers, Distributors, and Field Marshals. The Field Marshals are already deployed to the front lines of expanding God's Kingdom. They are called and committed to preaching and activating the Gospel of the Kingdom. They are constantly healing the sick, casting out devils, preaching God's salvation to hungry souls, multiplying churches, caring for the poor, and transforming society. Most of them are doing an outstanding job, but virtually all have a ceiling that keeps them from doing all that they are capable of, and that ceiling is almost always money! It is the responsibility of the other three links in the chain to see that this ceiling is removed.

The first link, the Providers, must already be in place as well. I don't think that God would have given us the word that funds will be released unless the wealth was actually there, and that would obviously be in the hands of the Providers. Undoubtedly, more Providers will be added, and many existing Providers will generate much more wealth, but the initial amount must currently be in place.

I am personally most interested in the Distributors link because that is where I feel I have a role. There are two kinds of distributors, Narrow-Band Distributors and Wide-Band Distributors. If the link was divided in two, the Narrow-Band Distributors would be toward the right, in direct contact with the Field Marshals. Ché Ahn, John Arnott, Bill Johnson, and Heidi Baker would be Narrow-Band Distributors because they each oversee networks of Field Marshals. When Ché Ahn receives funds, for instance, he will not distribute those funds to the

American Bible Society or the Southern Baptist International Mission Board or Wycliffe Bible Translators, worthy as those ministries may be. Ché is responsible under God for his own apostolic sphere that is represented by Harvest International Ministry. His Kingdom-oriented apostolic infrastructure is poised to make good use of huge amounts of wealth for God's causes.

Wide-Band Distributors would be toward the left side of the Distributor link, in direct touch with the Managers link on one hand, and with the Narrow-Band Distributors on the other. This is where I would locate myself. I do not have a network of Field Marshals, but I am networked with hundreds of active apostles, a good many of whom are Narrow-Band Distributors overseeing Field Marshals in virtually every part of the world. My role in distributing the wealth that is being transferred will be to get it into the hands of Kingdom-minded apostles who will know exactly what to do with it.

I now have established the necessary infrastructure to implement this Wide-Band Distribution in a responsible way with organizations such as the Global Distribution Network and The Hamilton Group, named in honor of Alexander Hamilton, who was my four-times great grandfather. Hamilton, as you may recall, was our first secretary of the Treasury, and he laid the foundation for the American financial system. We want our Kingdom distribution structure to reflect the creativity and the integrity of its namesake.

Ministry Revenue Funds

I now want to address the second link in the chain, that is, Managers. At the moment, this is our weakest link, and I wouldn't be surprised if God might be delaying the great transfer of wealth until we strengthen this link. The general idea is that the Managers multiply wealth that originates with the Providers before it goes further down the chain. For example, if a Provider releases $100,000, it would be nice if it were $300,000 by the time it got to the Distributors. The multiplication difference would be due to the Managers.

My vision is that we begin to shift our ministries and international apostolic networks from our current donor-based funding to revenue-based funding. In our traditional procedure, Narrow-Band Distributors—let's call them ministry leaders—have relied on donations from Providers to sustain their ministries. They have mailing lists. They assign staff members to "donor development." They know Providers who are attracted to their ministry and who will respond to appeals for cash flow or special projects. They spend their money well and thereby maintain the trust of the Providers. When a new need arises, they go back to the Providers, some of whom function like ministry ATMs. This donor-based system of funding has worked fairly well in the past, but I personally sense a change coming. I am in direct touch with several ministries that are finding that donor-based funding is not as productive as it once was.

A substantial step forward would be for ministries and apostolic networks to establish ministry revenue funds that would bring the Manager link more directly into the picture. In other words, a Provider would not only donate to a ministry's cash flow or special projects, all of which would be spent as expected, but would also contribute principal to a fund that would not be spent but managed. The proceeds from this revenue fund would then be available for cash flow or projects. Ideally the revenue fund would become large enough to provide the income needed to cover the annual administrative costs of the ministry initially and then be available for projects and expansion. Many will recognize that universities and other institutions have functioned this way with endowment funds for a long time. I personally feel that it is better to avoid the traditional term endowment for our Kingdom purposes because of some baggage that may come with it. "Ministry revenue fund" will work.

MANAGING MONEY IS BIBLICAL

In order for ministry revenue funds to accomplish their purpose, they must not only be managed, but they must be successfully managed. That means that we should shoot for a rate of return that is well above what has been considered as normal in the industry.

I have spent a good bit of time revisiting Jesus' well-known parables in Matthew 25 and Luke 19 that deal with talents and minas. First, we need to get rid of the common allegorical interpretation that in these parables Jesus is instructing us to use our personal gifts and abilities and talents in such a way that will please Him. No. These parables are dealing with finances and financial markets. The talent was a monetary instrument worth around $1 million and the mina was worth around $10,000. In each parable, the workers were instructed by the CEO to trade the money entrusted to them. In Luke 19:15 we are specifically told that the earnings came from "trading," the Greek for which is *diapragmateuomai*, a technical term from the financial industry of the day. Notice that the returns did not come from the restaurant business or from real estate or from imports/exports or from manufacturing but from managing money. This directly relates to the second link of the chain of wealth transfer.

We do not know what kind of financial trading they did, but a reasonable case can be made that it could have been a foreign currency exchange. In any case, the returns were considerably above what we consider normal in the industry. In Matthew they were 100 percent, and in Luke 500 percent and 1000 percent. Over what period of time did this return occur? Over the time it took for the CEO to take a trip and return. Since few trips take as much as a year, it could well be that they were annual rates of return or better. I am not sure we could expect rates of return near these for our ministry revenue funds today, but let's keep in mind that they are biblical!

Let me summarize what I have just said. If we are going to generate the massive financing required for reformation of society, we will need all four links of the chain of wealth transfer in action, and the weakest one at this writing is that of Managers. This is the time for Kingdom-minded financial managers to step up to the plate and move the whole Kingdom of God forward. They will be functioning as apostles or equivalent leaders in the Business Mountain, and their ministry will be just as important for the Kingdom as pastoring a church or going to the mission field or traveling as an evangelist. Did you notice that I used the word ministry? I am convinced that true biblical ministry happens in the workplace through those who are making money for the Kingdom just as much as it does through those who are, for example, writing spiritual songs and leading congregations in worship.

Mechanisms for Wealth Transfer

There are three ways that we can expect to see wealth transferred into the Kingdom of God. It is important to observe the big picture so as not to fall into the trap of highlighting just one of these mechanisms, as though it were the only way that God would choose to work.

Supernatural Transfer

God arranges circumstances so that wealth is entrusted to Distributors or Field Marshals without any overt action on their part. A biblical example of this is the Israelites leaving Egypt. When they got to the desert they were prosperous, and they didn't get their money from making bricks without straw. God had moved supernaturally in the hearts of the idol-worshiping

Egyptians to turn huge amounts of wealth over to God's people. In our day, the $1.5 billion gift from Joan Kroc to the Salvation Army was not generated from ringing bells over kettles at Christmas time, but it was a supernatural transfer.

Power to Get Wealth

Deuteronomy 8:18 says, "You shall remember the Lord your God, for it is He who gives you power to get wealth, that He may establish His covenant...." Here the responsibility for gaining wealth falls on the individual to whom God gives supernatural power for extraordinary increase. One way of paraphrasing this Scripture is to hear God saying: "I'm assigning you the responsibility to be prosperous so that you can fund My Kingdom." The more Kingdom-minded believers who become wealthy, the faster God's Kingdom will expand.

A Combination of the Two

Going back to the Israelites leaving Egypt, the supernatural transfer of wealth was accomplished by a seldom-recognized factor: the women! Exodus 3:22 says, "But every woman shall ask of her neighbor...articles of silver, articles of gold.... So shall you plunder the Egyptians." God gave the women extraordinary power to get wealth from their Egyptian neighbors, and apparently it wouldn't have happened without them. Even today, some large amounts of supernatural funding will be available only if we see ourselves as being assigned fiscal responsibility and if we determine to take the proper steps to secure the funding, even when it may come from unusual sources or through unusual means.

THE HAMILTON GROUP

Keeping in mind what I have just said, I have recently joined with some friends and formed an organization that is poised to receive and distribute whatever quantities of wealth God desires to release. When I described the Distributors link in the chain of wealth transfer, I mentioned The Hamilton Group (THG), named after my ancestor, Alexander Hamilton. My vision statement for THG is "Sophisticated Philanthropy for Apostolic Distribution." The first part, sophisticated philanthropy, a term I am borrowing from Bruce Cook,[1] means philanthropy specifically directed toward worthwhile goals, in this case extending God's Kingdom. Amazingly, some philanthropists evaluate their success only on how much they give, not on how much good their money might or might not be doing. THG, to the contrary, strictly monitors and audits whatever grants it makes.

The second part, for apostolic distribution, means that those who oversee and prioritize those Field Marshals who would qualify to receive funding are recognized and experienced apostles. They understand the Dominion Mandate, and they have efficient international administrative structures in place to use Kingdom funding responsibly. Some philanthropic agencies operate from a "seeker" mode. They seek funds through fund-raising departments, and they seek projects through research departments. Conversely, THG operates from a "server" mode. It serves Providers who desire a trustworthy infrastructure to distribute their Kingdom funds, and it serves the apostles who already have Kingdom-advancing projects in place all over the world and who will responsibly monitor their progress.

RECEIVING KINGDOM PROSPERITY

I believe that each one of us should desire prosperity, should pray for prosperity, and should expect that God will prosper us. Why? What does my prosperity have to do with the Kingdom of God? The answer is quite simple. If you're Kingdom-minded, you are attuned to philanthropy because the root meaning of philanthropy is "loving people." You want to help other people as much as you can. But you cannot help others with what you do not have. If you are struggling through life with mere sufficiency, you must use all you have for personal survival. However, the richer you are, the more you can provide for the Kingdom.

I like author Frank Damazio's plea that we all seek to be "surplus people." He says:

> Surplus living is a biblical concept taught by Christ and the apostles. Surplus is a kingdom principle…Surplus is more than is required or needed—over and above the norm. Surplus spills over the top. It is more than sufficient. It is excessive, beyond what you have expected.[2]

He then goes on to say,

> Prosperity begins with your decision to believe that God desires to use you to bless others and that to do so means you must have more than enough—you must have an overflow, a surplus, an abundance.[3]

Satan will do all he can to block such thinking from your mind and from your spirit. Satan is the author of poverty, and he will send the spirit of poverty that I mentioned earlier to keep you from receiving all that God has for you. He will even try to make you think that Jesus was poor, which is far from reality. Poverty is not a sign of spirituality or Christ-likeness. Instead of being oppressed by the spirit of poverty, move in the opposite spirit, which is the spirit of prosperity. Freedom in Christ means freedom to receive the abundance that God has reserved for you.

Four Steps Toward Godly Prosperity

Those who agree with what I have just said will be asking, "What steps do I need to take to, as rapidly as possible, become a surplus person who can help finance the advance of the Kingdom of God?" First, pray hard and ask God for a practical answer to the question that is tailor-made to your particular position in life. You are one of a kind. As you do this, simultaneously follow these four steps as much as you possibly can:

1. Listen to the prophets. Identify some who are respected and experienced prophets in the Body of

Christ. Get as near to them as you can. If possible, become personal friends with them. Be on the alert for guidance that God may give to you through them. The Bible says, "...Believe in the Lord your God and you shall be established; believe His prophets, and you shall prosper" (2 Chron. 20:20). As I have discovered in my own personal life, prophets often hold the keys to prosperity for us.

2. Delight in the law of the Lord. Delighting in God's law means that you deeply desire to please Him and obey Him in all things. God's Word provides the compass for every phase of your life. Some refer to this as recognizing the Lordship of Christ. Psalm 1 begins by saying that the person who delights in the law of the Lord is "like a tree planted by the rivers of water" and "whatever he does shall prosper" (Ps. 1:3). If you walk closely with God, He will make you a surplus person.

3. Confess all known sins. Look at what the Bible says: "He who covers his sins will not prosper, but whoever confesses and forsakes them will have mercy" (Prov. 28:13). This warning brings up a possible blockage to the abundance that God desires to pour out. Do a spiritual inventory and be honest with yourself. Is there anything in the past that you haven't dealt with? Or even worse, do you have "issues" in the present that you keep sweeping under the rug? If so, now is

the time to confess them and forsake them. It will open the door to prosperity.

4. Follow John Wesley's advice. Here is one of the most famous quotes from John Wesley. It is so clear that it needs no explanation. If you do what Wesley says, you can expect God to help you become a surplus person who has resources for advancing the Kingdom of God:

- Earn all you can.
- Save all you can.
- Give all you can.[4]

Open the Gates by Giving

Wesley's third admonition was "Give all you can." Let's look more closely at that for a moment. Earlier I mentioned Isaiah 60 where it says, "Your gates shall be open continually." If you want God to open the gates of prosperity in your life, you must be a giving person, and you must give cheerfully. Think hard about this word from the Lord: "There is one who scatters, yet increases more; and there is one who withholds more than is right, but it leads to poverty. The generous soul will be made rich…" (Prov. 11:24-25 NKJV). Why wouldn't God want you rich? He for sure doesn't want you poor. He doesn't want you to just scrape by with bare sufficiency for your own needs. The richer you are, the more you can do your part to finance the advance of the Kingdom and the reformation of society.

But in order to get there, you must follow God's rules for giving. I acknowledge that there are different interpretations of the biblical material on giving, but I have personally come to the conclusion that if you are going to be a reformer you must give tithes, offerings, and firstfruits.

Tithes are clearly mandated by Scripture. My advice is to take Malachi 3 seriously as a word from God and not try to argue it away. It tells you that if you don't bring your tithes (10 percent of your income) to God's storehouse, you are robbing God! But if you do tithe, God will open the windows of Heaven and pour out blessing. I shy away from legalism, but I interpret the tithe literally, and I strictly and consistently practice it in my own life.

Offerings are what you give over and above your tithe. They are also mentioned in Malachi 3:8. Tithes are not your money; you are giving God back His 10 percent. Offerings, then, are your own money that you are giving to God and His Kingdom. Be generous with offerings over and above your tithe.

Firstfruits represent a special kind of giving over and beyond tithes and offerings. Numbers 18 contrasts firstfruits and tithes. Tithes were for the Levites, and firstfruits were for the priests. In modern language, tithes are for the pastors or the storehouse, and firstfruits are for the apostles. Firstfruits, the first and the best, are given by faith at the beginning of the harvest, and tithes are returned to God after the harvest. Do you want to prosper? "Honor the Lord with your possessions, and with the firstfruits of all your increase; so your barns will be filled with plenty, and your vats will overflow with new wine" (Prov. 3:9-10 NKJV).

Kingdom-Minded Reformers

It will take money to finance the reformation. God wants this money in the hands of Kingdom-minded reformers. Do you want to be part of that company? If any of us says yes to that question, here is a checklist of our required characteristics:

We obey the Lord. We are sons and daughters of our heavenly Father, and our deepest desire is to do His will. Our lives will be holy, free from blemish, reproach, or blame.

We step out in faith. We believe and do not doubt. Skepticism will not creep in. Worry and fear have no place in our minds or in our hearts.

We give extravagantly. "He who sows sparingly will also reap sparingly, and he who sows bountifully will also reap bountifully" (2 Cor. 9:6 NKJV).

We humble ourselves. We acknowledge that all that we are and all that we possess are by God's grace. We refuse to become self-reliant and say, "My power and the might of my hand have gained me this wealth" (Deut. 8:17 NKJV).

We keep the true goal in sight. We focus on the Kingdom of God. "Your kingdom come. Your will be done on earth as it is in heaven" (Matt. 6:10 NKJV).

Endnotes

1. Bruce Cook, "The Psychology of Investing," *Fund Raising Management* 29, no. 1 (March 1998).

2. Frank Damazio, *The Attitude of Faith* (New Kensington, PA: Whitaker House, 2009), 133.

3. Ibid., 154.

4. John Wesley, "Serving God with Mammon," qtd. in Elesha Coffman, *Christianity Today*, November 1, 2001.

CULTURAL TRANSFORMATION
IS THE PRECURSOR TO
CULTURAL REFORMATION,
AND WE MUST HAVE A
MIGHTY REFORMATION IF WE
HOPE TO SEE LONG-LASTING
CHANGE IN OUR WORLD. WE
NEED A HOLY REVOLUTION
THAT INSPIRES DIVINE
INFRASTRUCTURE TO SUSTAIN
SPIRITUAL REFORMATION.

❧ 5 ❧

DRIVEN BY PRAYER: A PARADIGM SHIFT

Ché Ahn

One of the greatest keys to bringing God's will to the earth is prayer.

Billy Graham once said there are three keys to his crusades: Prayer. Prayer. And prayer.[1] John Wesley asserted, "God does nothing on earth save in answer to believing prayer."[2]

I couldn't agree more.

All that God has done at Harvest Rock Church is a direct result of prayer. Every story I will reveal has the same basis. Prayer is one way we give over to God what is rightfully His: results!

I have actually heard some people say that the renewal, which has been apparent since the mid-1990s, hit the world sovereignly, without prayer. I understand why people might say this. The Toronto group, for example, had not held any unusual prayer sessions before the Holy Spirit fell on January 20, 1994. To my knowledge, neither had the Anaheim Vineyard.

I believe, however, the Holy Spirit always falls in answer to prayer. I agree with what one leader said: "There has never been a historic revival without extraordinary prayer." These visitations of the last 15 or more years are most likely a result of all the fervent prayers the Body of Christ offered during the 1980s and early 1990s.

Although the Church as a whole did not see much fruit during the decade preceding the outpouring, one thing it did do was pray. The same was true for us. At least we prayed, especially my friend Lou Engle.

An Incomparable Intercessor

My mentor and professor, Dr. C. Peter Wagner, once said that if he were going to plant a church, the first person he would recruit would be an intercessor.

By God's grace, I did not need to recruit one. God had already joined me with Lou Engle, an incomparable intercessor. Lou is far more than a prayer warrior who oversees intercession in our church. He has been a loyal friend, confidant, and prophet—to me, Harvest Rock Church, and the apostolic network I am privileged to lead (Harvest International Ministry).

In fact, Lou reminds me of Frank Bartleman, a revivalist who gave himself to fasting and prayer during the Azusa Street

Revival in 1906. I have never met anyone who embodies and personifies prayer as does Lou Engle. In fact, that very DNA is what led him to father TheCall. This innovative outreach has now become a worldwide prayer movement to tear down the wicked strongholds of society and to contend for global revival. Many tangible, life-changing results can be attributed directly to the events or "Calls" held all over the world.

Extraordinary Prayer

Renowned 18th-century theologian Jonathan Edwards said that if you want to experience revival, there must be "explicit agreement, visible union and extraordinary prayer."[3]

A trail of such prayer pervades the accounts of what has happened at Harvest Rock Church. Persistence has born results; as Alice Smith puts it today, "Pray until something happens."[4]

When we began Harvest Rock Church, we started as a prayer meeting. When we heard from God to go into protracted revival meetings, we began the first 21 days with praying and fasting. That was the first time I had been on a 21-day liquid fast. We met five days a week for prayer, and in the evenings we had revival meetings.

It is hard to believe that during the decade of the 1990s we hosted one of the longest revival meetings in the world. Toronto Airport Christian Fellowship and Brownsville Assemblies of God hosted similar revivals as well—along with more short-lived "hot spots" comparable to the most recent Lakeland Revival and other "zones" found around the globe.

I firmly believe that the enduring quality of our revival stems from the fact that we devote, dedicate, and sustain the meetings through prayer.

Continuous Prayer

A key development in the life of our church came in the fall of 1995. The Lord began to impress upon Lou Engle that we should establish a Twenty-Four-Hour House of Prayer for All Nations. For years, Lou wanted to establish this kind of sustained prayer, but the timing wasn't right. Now, the Lord was giving us permission to do it.

We held a meeting of hand-picked intercessors and shared the vision of holding around-the-clock prayer. Each day was divided into three-hour shifts from which intercessors could select a single three-hour shift each week. They committed to whatever time slot they chose and could invite anyone they desired to join them in prayer during that time.

Lou was also inspired to create a clear job description and outline of what needed to be covered during each shift. A special room was devoted exclusively to continual prayer. It contained a map of the world covering a full wall. The carpet was extra thick, with kneeling rails, pillows, and a variety of chairs. The shelves were filled with quality testimonies and materials about prayer and world missions.

New journals were regularly placed in the room to cover current prayer requests and answers; record prophecies, revelations, and dreams; and list the names of those from our midst who were involved in ministry around the world. A wide selection of praise and worship music and a small stereo completed the simple furnishings.

During each session, there would be intimate worship and praise, as well as many styles of prayer covering many topics as the Spirit led.

To inaugurate the prayer room, we decided to call our church to an extended time of praying and fasting for the first 40 days of 1996. During this time, Lou personally baptized the room by praying and fasting for 40 days. For the final ten days of his fast, Lou literally lived in the prayer room and prayed without ceasing. He only left to walk across the street to his home to shower and change clothes.

After the 40 days were completed, prayer shifts began in earnest. We cried out for our missionaries; we pled for nations; we made declarations over Hollywood and the youth of our country; we interceded for the government; and we invoked the Lord for revival. There was no end to all that was prayed and is still being prayed.

Some would literally place their hands on the map covering the wall and pray for different nations. Others would weep and whisper in tongues. Some shifts were like a military drill, with the directives of God being "issued" in the Spirit realm. It was new for us to have such intensive prayer going forth at all times. But as we have seen, it is where the Lord is inviting many to participate.

We now find that throughout the world, the Lord is prompting perhaps thousands of ministries to host 24/7 prayer and worship to the Lord. As we find ourselves in these last days, God is glorifying His name day and night throughout the whole earth. As the prayers rise as incense before God's altar through the conduits of those who will give themselves to prayer and worship, I have no doubt the atmosphere of the earth is being changed into the atmosphere of Heaven.

I don't know where we would be as a church, where Harvest International would be as a ministry, or where our staff would be as leaders if the intercessors had not given and did not continue to give of themselves in prayer. I believe intercessors are in one of the most critical positions of honor and value in God's Kingdom, and I want to thank again every person who has been involved with us in prayer over the years. You are truly Kingdom builders, and your reward will be abundant in Heaven! (See Matthew 6:33.)

As Rick Joyner wrote of his vision of Heaven:

> Those closest to the throne of God were those who gave themselves to intercession on earth....As I approached the Judgment Seat of Christ, those in the highest ranks were also sitting on thrones that were all a part of His throne...it seemed that faithful, praying

> women and mothers occupied more thrones
> than any other single group.[5]

I believe this is so. Many people feel they don't have a "full-time ministry," but we all do—it is never ceasing to pray. Some of the most faithful with this mandate throughout the ages have been mothers and grandmothers to whom prayer is continuous as they go about raising the next godly generation. God asks us to "give Him no rest till He establishes Jerusalem and makes her the praise of the earth" (Isa. 62:7 NIV 1984). We are all included in that directive.

The Moravians, unparalleled reformers and catalysts of revival and missions centuries ago, held continuous prayer sessions for more than 100 years. We would like to experience continuous prayer until the Lord returns. It may take on various forms and timelines over the years, but until the Kingdom is preached to all nations, we shall not cease to live a lifestyle of fasting and prayer (see Matt. 24:14).

Although not everyone is called to establish a Twenty-Four-Hour House of Prayer for All Nations, we can all do something. Perhaps 24/7 prayer can be done for a season, with church members signing up for time slots and praying from home so that all hours of the day are covered. God has led many churches to sponsor a weekly all-night prayer meeting. Surely regular corporate prayer meetings are vital. Some have joined with other churches (one group has more than 25 churches citywide) to have 24-hour worship and prayer for the city.

The important thing is to do what you believe the Father is showing you to do in regard to prayer and to "follow the cloud" as He leads you.

FORTY DAYS OF PRAYER AND FASTING

Lou Engle "takes the cake" (a poor analogy, perhaps) for completing the most 40-day fasts of any man I know. I jokingly say that I originally hired Lou to be on staff to do the fasting while I do the eating. Since Lou has recently moved out from our direct staff to his own wider ministry, the local prayer and fasting ball is now squarely back in my court.

Quite frankly, I really do not like to fast. In fact, I used to think I didn't need to fast. My wife Sue (one of the pastors of Harvest Rock Church) is another person who has given herself to prayer and fasting. I had reasoned that between Sue and Lou's dedication the whole church and I were covered, but I was wrong.

In the latter part of 1996, God began to confront me about an extended fast. Like many people, I had read Bill Bright's book about fasting, *The Coming Revival*. In it, Bright contends:

> The power of fasting as it relates to prayer is the spiritual atomic bomb of our moment in history to bring down the strongholds of evil, bring a great revival and spiritual awakening to America, and accelerate the fulfillment of the Great Commission.[6]

The second thing that God did was convict me through the writings of C. Peter Wagner on prayer. He wrote a six-volume series called The Prayer Warrior Series. His most recent book on prayer, *Praying with Power,* sums up the point that convinced me that I could not just rely on Lou or Sue. Instead, as the Senior Pastor of Harvest Rock, I had to lead.

> If the church is ever to become a house of prayer, the senior pastor must cast the vision and assume the leadership of the church's prayer ministry. That does not mean that the pastor cannot delegate the administration and the implementation of the prayer ministry... all the church members should know without question that their pastor has prioritized prayer in his or her personal life and ministry.[7]

Today, I couldn't agree more with Peter. The Lord began to speak to me that we as a pastoral staff should go on a 40-day fast together in 1997. We had heard about the pastors and churches in Houston fasting the last 40 days of 1996. City leader Doug Stringer of Someone Cares Houston led the fast. (You know it must be God's doing when people fast through Thanksgiving and Christmas!) John Arnott had also shared with me that his church in Toronto was planning a corporate fast the first 40 days of 1997. I heard that some 50 pastors and their churches in Dallas were planning to do the same thing. We decided our fast would begin one week after Lent and culminate 40 days later, on Easter Sunday.

That January, I shared the idea with the church, noting that we were committed to the fast as a pastoral staff and anyone who so desired could join us. To my amazement, more than 600 people made a commitment to participate in the fast in some way. Many people went on a vegetable fast, others ate one meal a day, and so on. More than 65 people engaged in a liquid fast for the entire 40 days. I was one of them.

Initially, I had a hard time. I was used to drinking diet Coke, so for the first three days I suffered caffeine withdrawal and experienced headaches and fatigue. The second week I dreamed of food almost nightly. I remember one dream very well: I came home and I saw a bowl of rice and a plate of Korean barbecue on the table. The dream seemed so real. I sat down and devoured the food. Then I realized I had broken my fast. I felt terrible about it. I felt like Esau who had given over his birthright for some measly food. Then I realized there was nothing I could do because I had already broken the fast, so I decided I should eat more. I had another helping. When I woke up, I realized it was only a dream. I was so grateful!

I think the dream motivated me and helped me not to break the fast even when I was tempted to do so. There is one practical note I would like to share concerning extended fasting: I was losing more muscle mass than body fat. After ten days, a physician in our church warned me to drink some liquid protein and to do some light exercise. That was vital advice for my health. Soon I began to lose body fat and not muscle. Use wisdom and consider your physician's advice about fasting. This is an especially important tip for those who regularly engage in extended fasts to maintain their body health. Of course, if the Lord has clearly spoken to you differently, follow His lead.

Even though most people lose weight fasting, that is not the reason for the fast. My main goal was to grow in love—a prayer that God is still answering in many wonderful ways.

We concluded the 40 days of fasting by conducting a healing conference. Mahesh Chavda was invited to be with us. On Friday night, he led us in a "prayer watch," which is essentially an all-night prayer meeting. Around three in the morning, a most unusual thing happened. A huge tree in front of the auditorium split in half, as if struck by lightning. It happened to be right in front of my parking place! There was no wind, no rain, no lightning or any other natural cause for such an occurrence!

Someone who was leaving the prayer meeting reported what happened. When I shared it with Mahesh, he thought it was a sign that demonic strongholds were broken and that we would now see a greater release of the Holy Spirit. Mahesh had witnessed this kind of thing several times during his crusades in Africa. He told us that many times God would break the spirit of witchcraft by splitting a tree, usually by lightning. Most often, the local witches knew that particular tree as a power source. Whether that applies to this particular incident or not, I do believe God was giving us a sign to encourage us that we were right on track through our obedience in fasting and prayer. It is filled with power! As many who fast say, the results are seldom seen during the fast, but quite often seen after you are finished. Don't give up, and don't look with your natural eyes for the results. You are changing the spiritual climate!

The Fruit of Prayer

Most likely, none of us will know the full effect of our intercession in this life until we get to Heaven. We do, however, know of several things that happened in our city that we believe were influenced greatly by our prayers and that of many others in the days and months that followed this first extended fast of Harvest Rock Church.

One was a dramatic name change for an important public landmark. Lou Engle gives this account of what happened:

> Protecting the original water source of Pasadena and Los Angeles is a dam bearing the name of Devil's Gate. My fellow intercessors and I sensed strongly that such a name literally brought a curse on the city.
>
> A 1947 local newspaper article said, "It's true Devil's Gate is named because of the resemblance of the rocks to his satanic majesty." One night, I awoke from a dream with these words spoken to me: "Go and pour the salt of your purity on it." I didn't know what this word pertained to at that moment, but prior to coming to Pasadena, the Lord had given me a word from the passage where Elisha poured salt into

the water source of Jericho and healed the contaminated waters (see 2 Kings 2:19-22).

That morning in a prayer meeting, an intercessor in our church prayed that God would change the name of Devil's Gate. Then it struck me with much force to go and pour salt into the stream at Devil's Gate as an act of prophetic intercession—and ask the Lord to change the name, break the curse, and let the rivers of revival flow bringing fruitfulness to the Los Angeles Valley. We took our Greater Pasadena for Christ intercession team to the dam and did precisely that. At that time, Southern California had been experiencing a severe drought of five years' duration. I know thousands of other Californians were praying for rain as well, but God encouraged us when eight days later it began to rain. The rains were so heavy the newspapers called it a "Miracle March." It was astonishing. We pondered this. Could it be a sign of renewal and revival—first the natural, then the spiritual?

However, for two years, the name of the dam remained the same. One of our intercessors went to God to inquire again. He spoke to her that the name would be changed, and it would be an Indian name. Soon after, a Los Angeles Times newspaper article added to our excitement of answered prayer when it spoke of a name change for the dam: Hahamongna. That's the name the Gabrielinos (early Pasadena Indians) gave to what now is known as Devil's Gate, the 250-acre area at the north end of the Arroyo Seco....The English language translation is "Flowing Waters: Fruitful Valley." Nearly everyone agrees that Hahamongna will be a more appropriate name for this long-neglected community asset after it is restored to its natural state....

"Flowing rivers and a fruitful valley"—that is our intercession now, and what has begun since the outpouring began in 1994.[8]

Another major turnaround we witnessed in our city was the repentance and conversion of a major cult. Many people have no doubt heard of the Worldwide Church of God (WCG) or its magazine *The Plain Truth*. In the early days of their being headquartered in Pasadena, we believed this cult was a major demonic stronghold in our city, and we repeatedly prayed and lifted them up.

I am not saying we were the reason the WCG changed, but we may have played a part. God had been working on the organization for quite some time. I know many former members who had become Christians and were fervently interceding for WCG. I do believe, however, the many collective prayers, including ours, were responsible for a radical transformation.

I remember hearing Jack Hayford say, "To my knowledge, never has a cult turned around so dramatically in the history of Christianity." Today, the WCG is a member of the National Association of Evangelicals. I now know many of the leaders personally, including Joseph Tkach, the president of the WCG. I honestly can say they are true brothers in Christ. (If God can bring down the walls of deception of the WCG through the prayers of the saints, then we need to be earnest in faith and prayer that the scales of deception also fall from groups such as the Mormons and the Muslims.)

It never occurred to me how WCG would come back around into my life again just a few years later. As realigning took place throughout the Worldwide Church of God, they decided they would no longer maintain their world headquarters campus in downtown Pasadena. Their auditorium, called the "Crown Jewel" of the city, was offered by special private sale—to us!

The home of Harvest Rock Church is now in the Ambassador Auditorium, which is an incredible miracle!

PERSEVERING IN PRAYER

I am ever so grateful about what the Lord has done in bringing renewal to our city. I believe the extended duration of this visitation added to the impact it has had upon multiplied thousands over the years. The full impact of the revival is not yet seen, but I believe it is coming.

There is a temptation to lose our fervency in prayer when things seem to be happening sovereignly. Instead, we have learned that when God pours out His unmerited grace, we should give ourselves to prayer as never before (see 1 Thess. 5:17). We need to give God no rest until multitudes are swept into the Kingdom and a radical transformation is seen in all areas of society.

As we receive this new strengthening and vision, we are beginning to slowly see more amazing and widespread change throughout the nations. God is raising up wise strategists such as Lance Wallnau and others to unfold how we can influence every "mountain of culture" by taking our place as believers and serving at the top of each mountain. This takes revival from salvation alone to societal transformation—the destination I am sure our King of all governments intends.

There is a further step beyond societal transformation: I believe this "final" goal is reformation. This is where we pray, work, infiltrate, and influence society until there is a firm infrastructure built to sustain God's values for the long term and cause them to replace man's "good ideas." As Alice Smith says in her book *Beyond the Veil*, "Burning, believing, prevailing, persuading, persevering, intimate prayer always precedes a move of God."[9]

To this end we continue to labor, pray, and believe! We must press forth until He makes His people a praise on the earth…and all of the kingdoms of this world have become the kingdoms of Christ! (See Revelation 11:15.)

Endnotes

1. Ché Ahn, *Fire Evangelism* (Grand Rapids, MI: Chosen Books, 2006), 107.

2. Dutch Sheets, *Intercessory Prayer* (Ventura, CA: Regal Books, 1996), 23.

3. "A Humble Attempt to Promote Explicit Agreement and Visible Union of God's People, in Extraordinary Prayer, for the Revival of Religion and the Advancement of Christ's Kingdom on Earth," *The Works of Jonathan Edwards*, vol. 2, from Christian Classic Ethereal Library.

4. Alice Smith, *Beyond the Veil* (Ventura, CA: Renew Books, 1997), 39.

5. Rick Joyner, *The Final Quest* (New Kensington, PA: Whitaker House, 1996), 116-117.

6. Bill Bright, *The Coming Revival* (Orlando: New Life Publications, 1995), 16.

7. C. Peter Wagner, *Praying with Power* (Shippensburg, PA: Destiny Image, 1997), 148-149.

8. Ché Ahn, *Into the Fire* (Ventura, CA: Renew Books, 1998), 104-105.

9. Smith, 2.

As we discover and embrace the mountains of society we are called to, our gifts, callings, and anointing will synergize to produce great breakthrough and favor to usher in the Kingdom of God.

≈ 6 ≈

GOD'S MEDIA ARMY

Patricia King

*The armies of heaven were following Him,
riding on white horses and dressed in fine
linen, white and clean*
(Revelation 19:14 NIV 1984).

In a natural war, the nation that conquers the air space has the greatest tactical advantage. In September 2004, I received an alarming dream in regards to a media army taking its position in this way. I saw God raising up a powerful media army, and many of its troops were young people. Also, apostles, prophets, evangelists, teachers, and pastors had changed roles so as to serve God in the media. This infantry also consisted of screenwriters, filmmakers, radio broadcasters, television producers, cameramen, editors, web media personnel, actors, actresses, and many others. All of them had come together to establish a critical and strategic position to conquer air space for the Lord.

Then, I saw a demonic media army raised up by the enemy to battle against this emerging, holy combatant force. In the dream, a council meeting in the second heaven led satan to dispatch his media army meant to thwart those Christians contending for the airwaves.

> *As for you, you were dead in your transgressions and sins, in which you used to live when you followed the ways of this world and of the ruler of the kingdom of the air, the spirit who is now at work in those who are disobedient* (Ephesians 2:1-2).

Attempting to claim its position in the airwaves is a demonic prince that desires to plague the nations with sinful darkness. The Lord, however, is raising up a mighty moving force to establish Kingdom authority in the airwaves. Responding to the media call in this hour is absolutely critical. We must win the battle!

OUR CALL INTO MEDIA

One evening in January 2003, I turned on the TV and it struck me that an unusual number of programs featuring New Age prophets, spirit mediums, psychics, and others operating in supernatural phenomena had flooded the programming options. One false prophet after another displayed "magic" and "spiritual gifts." Such displays vexed my soul. I thought to myself, *Lord where is the true prophetic in the midst of this counterfeit uprising? Where is Your voice, Father? Where is the prophetic Church on the airwaves?*

Secular media often dictates our culture's values. What is on the airwaves conditions the public's mindset. The media's magnetism is one reason why the darkness of immorality gets so widespread. Every single day, nearly every TV show, movie, and magazine somehow communicates that immorality and anti-Christian values are normal. The media has influenced us to believe that we should want what it puts on display. Much of the degradation, violence, rebellion, and perversity that our society struggles with results from the pervasive weight of the media's corrupted voice.

THE AIRWAVES BELONG TO THE LORD

God owns everything and we are to steward what He owns, and that includes the airwaves. When the Church abdicates its God-appointed position, our rightful place gets usurped and the airwaves are filled with unhealthy influences. It's not enough for us to complain about all the corruption and immorality on the air, or to simply turn off the TV in frustration; we must take our position back.

That evening in January 2003, the Lord convicted my heart to take personal responsibility for what so grieved me. He asked me if I would be willing to move forward in faith to raise a true prophetic standard amidst the counterfeit uprising. The position abdicated by the Church must be reclaimed. Was I willing to do something about it? Over the years, He has called many others. As a result of those faithful pioneers taking their places, a degree of Christian presence exists on today's airwaves. Much of today's Truth-based programming, however, is hidden inside of Christian networks and primarily structured around church services. All of this, of course, is valuable and possibly God-ordained, but what about the un-churched and the unsaved? How do we address the spiritually hungry who can't relate to how our messages are packaged in services? That evening, the Lord issued a personal challenge to me: "Would you take responsibility to do your part?"

I wondered to myself, *Is there a way we could relate more to all those lost souls who are searching and wanting something to fill the spiritual void, but are not interested in 'church culture'?* Was there a way to bring the Father's true prophetic to the spiritually hungry to give them a revelation of Christ? Bursting into prayer, I asked God to raise up the prophets He had prepared for such a task. That's when the Holy Spirit asked me, "Will you be part of the media army I am raising up? Will you go for Me?" My immediate response was, "No!"

I shared with the Holy Spirit all the reasons why I was a poor choice: I had no training in production; I never had any desire to be on TV; I had no money; and I had no team with any media experience. I did promise Him, however, that I would fervently pray for others to be raised up. That was when the Holy Spirit said, "Since when has your lack of ability, income, or team and resources been an issue?"

Right then, I told the Lord I would do whatever He wanted me to, and I would trust Him if He wanted me to produce a television program. "But," I added, "You're going to have to help me, because I don't have a clue where to begin."

Extreme Prophetic Television

I felt the Holy Spirit say, "Take this up as a prophetic mandate." He then gave me the strategy: Produce a program called *Extreme Prophetic* that would be filmed right in Hollywood, the birthplace of most programming that dictates many of the images and mindsets of society. The Lord said, "Go right to the jugular of the Babylonian system of the entertainment industry." In the Bible, the Babylonian system speaks of seduction, man's agenda, pride, and a worldly love of money. In other words, it's all about man's name and fame. Seductive evil spirits, such as Jezebel and Leviathan, lurk around the Babylonian kingdom seeking to destroy lives. Hollywood is controlled and influenced significantly by these two dark spirits. Over the years, many Christians have faithfully stood in the gap to dismantle this evil grip over the entertainment industry. As a result of their persevering faith, the Babylonian strongholds are coming down! Ministry gatherings like "TheCall: Hollywood" and other organized intercessory events and groups have literally broken ground and prepared the way.

The Lord required us to film in Hollywood and to put a stake in the ground that declared, "God's prophetic Church is here!" We were then directed to air the show in Las Vegas, a sin capital of the entertainment industry. The goal of this mandate was to raise up a prophetic intercessory standard against the Babylonian system with its false claim on that territory. At the same time, many other Christians were receiving similar mandates. Others had been forerunners in this area for many previous years. This call to broadcast was a prophetic, intercessory act. I thought it would be used to initiate increased prayer for the airwaves and to call forth more seasoned prophets to step up to the plate. Honestly, I didn't feel called to engage in any more production other than this one assignment. But even at that, I had no idea how to begin. I had the vision but no clue how to do it. So I prayed for help!

A couple of weeks later, I was speaking at a prophetic conference at Bill Johnson's church in Redding, California. During a break, a woman approached me and explained that she almost never attended Christian conferences and had never before approached a speaker. But the Holy Spirit told her to introduce herself to me. Her name was Shirley Ross and she had spent over 20 years in Hollywood working as a producer. She simply said that she believed that God wanted her to help me somehow. I thought, *Thank You, Jesus.*

I took Shirley to dinner and shared the vision God had given me for *Extreme Prophetic*. Right there, she offered to volunteer time to help put the production together. Now all we had to do was create the show. We had no money to work with, but Shirley managed to corral some volunteers; in six weeks, she put the whole shoot together for a fraction of what such a production would usually cost. God miraculously provided all the finances. In addition, over 300 intercessors signed up to pray daily for the program—it was just amazing!

In our first *Extreme Prophetic* production, Wesley and Stacey Campbell, Larry Randolph, Todd Bentley, and I went to Hollywood to be the guest prophets. Each prophet paid his or her own way and sowed time into the project. Filming was hilarious. Todd and Wesley were as natural as ever, but the cameras totally freaked out Stacey, Larry, and I, and all of us had pasted-on smiles. The make-up artist made us up like porcelain dolls and we didn't feel at all ourselves; this turned out to be a totally different environment than what we were used to.

After filming in Hollywood, we purchased airtime in Las Vegas on Warner Brothers Network and were placed between two popular New Age programs. The moment we booked our time, one of the New Age shows—which was hosted by a well-known spirit medium—canceled out. So, we took their slot. What a powerful prophetic statement: The Church was taking back ground! We aired our *Extreme Prophetic* programs for five weeks.

Fruit came immediately. One particular encouraging e-mail was written by an obvious sinner, as evidenced by swear words throughout the note. This man had been powerfully touched by the program and wanted to express his gratefulness. In addition to that, masses of believers seemed to be getting stirred up about taking true prophecy to the airwaves. We received tremendous affirmations from credible, well-known prophets and leaders in the Body of Christ. God's vision for bringing His true prophetic into public visibility through the airwaves was spreading like wildfire.

After successfully shooting and airing our programs, I thought we were finished with the assignment, but the Lord had a different plan: He confirmed that He wanted us to produce a weekly program. At that time, I had a more-than-full-time schedule as an itinerant speaker and ministry leader. I didn't know how I could possibly add in the production of a weekly program, but God had shown time and time again that He knew what He was doing, even if I didn't. So I agreed to continue, as did Shirley, who literally laid down her career to honor the Lord's call and serve the program. We had no money, no equipment, no staff, and no talent. But we did have the Lord, and He is always more than enough.

Every step of the way, we followed the Holy Spirit. Quite literally, He was our director. In one visitation, He told us that the program would appear, at first, as if wrapped in swaddling clothes. Our beginnings, like those of Christ, would be humble. But if we followed Him, He promised to cause us to influence people for His glory. God showed up every step of the way. He provided us with two cameras, microphones, a small lighting package, and an editing computer and program. Everywhere we went, He bathed us in favor. Individuals and organizations offered to help, a glorious team of intercessors was raised up, and we received our first financial partners. He was creating the *Extreme Prophetic* family. We had so much fun being completely reliant on the Holy Spirit.

When shooting began our weekly program, we couldn't afford the exorbitant sum to rent a studio. Instead, we shot in Shirley's condo as we sat at her kitchen table against a wall! We wanted our program to look different from shows that featured preachers behind pulpits or on staged sets. Well, that do-it-yourself, in the home "soundstage" certainly felt different from that! We had never worked a camera, set up lights, or done editing. All we knew to do was ask God for help and read the manuals. To finish shows, we often worked over 18 hours a day and 7 days a week. Many of our initial programs are now embarrassing to look at because of poor lighting, shaky cameras, bad sound, and weak transitions, but the Spirit's anointing was powerful and more than made up for our technical inexperience.

The Lord's faithfulness and favor kept showing up, and so did the kindness and blessings of visionaries like Dr. Dick and Joan Dewert and Brad Lockhart at the Miracle Channel in Canada. When we presented our program, they discerned its anointing and potential. Looking past the technical weaknesses, they took a chance on airing us, and did so during prime time all across Canada! Being favored like that was an amazing gift!

Through our website (www.extremeprophetic.com) and the Miracle Channel's (www.miraclechannel.ca), we began to stream *Extreme Prophetic* out to the nations. Letters, phone calls, and e-mails came in from all over the world. People from Canada, the United States, Israel, Croatia, Romania, Central America, Africa, Japan, Australia, New Zealand, and every continent wrote to tell how they had been touched by the show. Many people watched every week to see if we had a destiny word from the Lord specifically for them. One of our favorite reports came from a man of Muslim background who wrote us, "When I watched your program I felt mysteriously drawn by God. I found myself kneeling down and giving my heart to Jesus Christ." Amen!

Since that time, God has opened up other networks for airing and we have grown in relationship with a company of prophets who desire to bring light into the darkness through the airwaves. The prophetic community has been such a wonderful support. Men and women of God such as Bobby Conner, Paul Keith Davis, Heidi Baker, James Goll, Stacey Campbell, Cindy Jacobs, Graham Cooke, John Paul Jackson, Todd Bentley, and others have given us their blessings as well as personal interview time. Through the Elijah List, my good friend Steve Shultz has since launched a prophetic television network on the web and he interviews prophets carrying profound, critical messages. Thousands of viewers from around the world watch this web TV. Many others, like Wendy and Rory Alec from God TV, are claiming airwaves globally with a fresh prophetic authority.

THE MONEY DEMON

For the most part, secular media is controlled by money. As part of the Babylonian strategy, how much money you have usually determines whether or not you step into any form of media or not. When we began, someone told us not to start unless we had a million dollars. Well, at that point, we didn't even have a million cents, but we proceeded because of the Lord's direction and trusted Him one day at a time. In the beginning, one contract offered us money to produce the program but put controlling interest of *Extreme Prophetic* in the hands of investors. We felt the Lord restrain us from going that route; He made it clear that He wanted to raise up His own financial partners and enlist them as part of His volunteer media army.

When God called us to the media, I had been in public prophetic ministry for over 23 years. I had planted churches, worked in missions, and engaged in apostolic projects, but I had never experienced the financial pressure that I did when stepping into media. The warfare was actually tangible and, at times, the pressure was unbearable. To proceed, we needed more personnel, more sophisticated equipment, and more software than we actually had. Everything came with a huge price tag. If we didn't make the investment, then we couldn't upgrade our quality, which meant not being able to take more air space.

At one point, I remember feeling a heavy weight of demonic assault. I was overseas when I received word from our book-keeper who said, "The well is dry." We had no money left in our account and only had two weeks until the month's end to make our budget. I asked Shirley Ross to inform each staff member on the production team of our situation. Ron and I owned a small home that we could sell or mortgage to cover expenses for one month but after that we had nothing left of our own to invest. We could offer them the security of the current month's salary but could not promise anything beyond that. Although we were standing on the truth, we wanted them to know all the facts, should they need to find other employment. Our team members had families to care for and needed provision. We communicated the situation to every worker. After sharing, each individual stated that they were in *Extreme Prophetic* for the long haul; if we had no money for paychecks, they would trust God to meet their needs, even if that meant taking a second job.

David's Mighty Men

Just months before, these people had given up their secure employment positions and laid down businesses so as to pursue God's call on their lives. Now, they were being severely tested. I was reminded of David's mighty men (see 1 Chron. 11:10-19) who were willing to risk their well-being, and even their lives, to defend a field for their King. Our team members had committed to taking the airwaves for God. To see the Kingdom advance, they were willing to work long hours, receive no pay, and fight ferocious warfare. They remained focused and faithful as did our financial partners and intercessors!

We praise the Lord that His provision came through—at the final hour, but it was enough to meet everyone's needs. The testing of these difficult months proved the heart of God's servants. What prevailed was an opposite spirit to the Babylonian mindsets of greed, self-exaltation, and pride, and breakthroughs followed. The Lord promises to always give His people victory in Christ (see 2 Cor. 2:14). As we long as we don't lose faith, God's media army is going to win on every front. God is more than able to give us the territory so that He will be lifted up in the earth.

ANGELIC VISITATION

"Are they not all ministering spirits sent forth to minister for those who will inherit salvation?" (Heb. 1:14 NKJV). In our time, many people are receiving angelic visitation—it is one of the earmarks of harvest season. The Book of Acts is full of evidence of angelic assistance during harvest and persecution. If you desire to bring light into the darkness, be confident that angels will be assigned to protect, provide, strengthen, and bring communication to you. God's media army consists not only of those who are called in His Body, but also heavenly hosts who are there to support and encourage us. Increased angelic visitation will occur within the media. I have seen prophetic visions of angels, spiritual winds, and fires showing up on sets and during shoots. Amazing signs and wonders will accompany many of those who are walking with God in media mandates this season.

ARE YOU BEING CALLED?

God's media army is truly being raised up in this hour. Perhaps you are personally being recruited. He is calling intercessors, financial partners, technical and administrative support, creative directors, producers, and all sorts of individuals who are willing to stand for Him. He is looking for those who are set apart for His purposes, who are not compromised with love for money, fame, and power. He is calling those who love their King and, who like David's mighty men, are willing to defend the airwaves for Him. Gross darkness prevails in and through the airwaves, and the Lord wants His light bearers to invade the darkness. If your heart is beating with a call toward media, then pray for Him to pave the way for you. He is so good and will more than meet you as you step out in faith. Try praying the following prayer:

Dear Heavenly Father,

I commit myself wholly to You in spirit, soul, and body. I make myself available to serve You in any area of the media. I feel called to Your media army and I say "Yes!" All that I am and all that I have is Yours. Thank You, for Your abundant grace that enables me to do all things in Christ who strengthens me. Open the way and I will walk in it. I am ready to serve You by taking Your light into the darkness! In Jesus' name, Amen!

CONCLUSION

*Of the increase of His government and peace
there will be no end, upon the throne of
David and over His kingdom, to order it and
establish it with judgment and justice from
that time forward, even forever. The zeal of
the Lord of hosts will perform this*
(Isaiah 9:7).

Beloved, we are called to disciple the nations. When we display the goodness of God outside of the Church and in the worlds of politics, music, Hollywood, technology and medicine, we display the glory of the Lord and nonbelievers will be drawn to His light (see Isa. 60:1-3). As Lance Wallnau mentioned, you don't need to win every soul in a country to disciple a nation. In fact, it may be more effective to occupy the most influential seats of power, as they are what govern and dictate the morality and course of events in a country.

This book is filled with divine strategies to equip you to positively impact your world. As you read about the Seven

Mountains, you may have identified with one or more of them. What are you doing to influence your community? Prayerfully consider how God wants to involve you in discipling your own nation. Which facets of society are you called to influence?

When we dream with God, He partners and collaborates with us to bring His Kingdom into the highways and byways of our communities. We are to be salt and light to the world, to sustain our world with the divine breath of life and to bring godly revelation to people so that they might not perish for a lack of vision (see Prov. 29:18). The Good News that Jesus preached invites us into a holy and heavenly relationship with our Living God that can be experienced on earth. The Kingdom of God brings righteousness, peace, and joy wherever it goes (see Rom. 14:17). We are commissioned, dear friends, to bring God's justice, His peaceful presence, and His abundant joy into every home, every business, and every city in our world. Incline your ear to hear God's voice and press in to receive holy vision for how to accomplish His Great Commission with your life.

Lord, what area of society have You called me to influence? I yield my heart and mind to You, as You impart Your heart and vision to me. Lord, break my heart for what breaks Yours. Show me the opportunities that I have before me that I have not yet noticed. Give me strength and courage to step out in risk to minister to those around me.

Lord, teach me how to disciple my nation. I desire

greater wisdom and revelation to strategically win my neighbors, my leaders, and my culture to the Good News. I want to see Your special prayer come to pass— may Your Kingdom be on the earth as it is in Heaven.

Lord, I ask for dreams and visions that would spark holy passion in me. I am grateful that You share so much with me, for You have called me friend instead of servant (see John 15:15). Your Word says You reveal Your secrets to Your prophets (see Amos 3:7). Lord, reveal Your secrets to me. Unfold Your desires and plans for my city, my region, my state, and my country. How do I partner with You to bring Your Kingdom to the earth? Lord, I long to see the kingdoms of this world become Your Kingdoms. Teach me how to colabor with You to bring cultural transformation and reformation. I long to see Your Kingdom established in strength and longevity in the earth.

Lord, I yield myself to Your vision and to be used for Your purposes. Use me as powerfully as You can to make Your Kingdom come and Your will be done on the earth. Amen.

BIBLIOGRAPHY

Johnson, Bill. "Invading Babylon." In *Dreaming with God: Secrets to Redesigning Your World Through God's Creative Flow*, 87-109. Shippensburg: Destiny Image Publishers, 2006.

Wallnau, Lance. "The Seven Mountain Mandate." In *The Reformer's Pledge*, edited by Che Ahn et al., 177-194. Shippensburg: Destiny Image Publishers, 2010.

Vincent, Alan. "Occupying the Gates of the Heavenly City." In *The Kingdom at War*, 151-164. Shippensburg: Destiny Image Publishers, 2011.

Wagner, C. Peter. "Stewarding for Reformation." In *The Reformer's Pledge*, edited by Che Ahn et al., 195-213. Shippensburg: Destiny Image Publishers, 2010.

Ahn, Che. "Media Mania." In *Say Goodbye to Powerless Christianity*, 135-141. Shippensburg: Destiny Image Publishers, 2009.

King, Patricia. "God's Media Army." In *Light Belongs in the Darkness*, 157-167. Shippensburg: Destiny Image Publishers, 2005.